From Pillar
∞ *to* Post ∞

with best wishes
from

Angela Claysmith Jenkin

*Back cover painting 'The back of 45 South Street', 1967
by Angela Jenkins.*

From Pillar

to Post

Angela Claysmith Jenkins

HiP

HISTORY INTO PRINT

First published by
History into Print, 56 Alcester Road,
Studley, Warwickshire B80 7LG in 2007
www.history-into-print.com

ISBN 10: 1 85858 317 9
ISBN 13: 978 1 85858 317 4

A Cataloguing in Publication Record
for this title is available from the British Library

Typeset in New Baskerville
Printed in Great Britain by
Cromwell Press Ltd.

Contents

Chapter 1

⦿ Angela by name: angel by nature? ⦿

Naturally enough, I had no idea, when I was born, that I came from such an unconventional family. I didn't even suspect anything until I was about nineteen. Time passed, events happened, there were various family traumas like in any family and still, I had no idea. Eventually, when exchanging information at college about families, dates and home, I realised: something didn't fit. I needed some questions answered. The answers came slowly, over a period of forty years, and what a strange story it was.

I was born in May 1944, a wanted child, much loved and cared for by parents who adored each other. We lived in a big house on the main road at Astwood Bank, a village straddling the Ridgeway about four and a half miles from Redditch, in the county of Worcestershire.

Me aged 18 months.

If truth be told I can't remember much about my first four years, but Mum's testimony together with family photographs paint a picture of stability and normality. My eldest sister, Jean, was fourteen when I was born. My brother Jimmy was ten, and Rosemary was nine.

After my birth Granny Winnett, Mum's mother, used to come up for the day to help with the washing and housework. Dad would drive the four miles to Alcester to collect her, and once Gran had checked on Mum and her latest grand-daughter she would get on with the washing. Granny had taken over this job when I was two weeks old. Until then Mrs. Aubrey had come for two mornings a week to look after Mum, do the nappies, then the other washing and a bit of dusting.

Anyway, Gran would do the washing in the galvanised boiler with the gas ring underneath to heat the water. Once the washing was on the line she would start the cleaning. There were no fitted carpets but the big carpet squares in each room and all the runners had to be done with the Ewbank. The stained floorboards were dusted and polished up with a dry mop that had a triangular head with red cotton fringes to get in all the corners.

Sometimes my brother and sisters were allowed to take me out in my big smart pram. They would take me down the lanes behind the house leading to the ancient village of Feckenham, the centre of an early medieval forest. Occasionally they would bump me across the road to the playground on the top of Fox's Hill, and once I was tipped up and hung from the straps of my harness.

Our house was rambling and down the outside of it was a wide passage which led to a big yard. This yard fronted workshops which extended to a factory. Originally needles were manufactured there but now knitted clothes were the product. Inside the house the rooms were lofty and had picture rails and huge skirting boards. The panelled doors had brass knobs and looked very smart with their new coat of paint.

My parents were pleased with their house and bought oddments of stylish second-hand furniture whenever they could. One such item was a mahogany side table with thick barley-twist legs and rail across the front on the edge of a hidden drawer. They paid five shillings (twenty five pence) for it at Little's shop in Headless Cross. Mum still has this desk table and one day it will be mine.

When I was a few months old my parents decided we would go by train to visit Grandma Ancell, Auntie Stella and Uncle David in Doncaster where they lived near the airforce camp. Preparations were made and we boarded the train leaving the pride and joy – my swish new pram – ready to be loaded into the goods van. As we steamed out of the station Mum saw it still on the platform, forgotten! By the time it had been forwarded to Doncaster our holiday was over and I never had my moment of glory in my swanky pram.

Jean left school when she was fifteen and worked at Shrimpton and Fletcher's needle factory. After about six months she left and went to Lapworth near Birmingham to live with a family and look after their children. Mrs. Flood our local health visitor persuaded her, during a visit home, to begin training as a Nursery Nurse when she was sixteen.

When I was about two years old Mum and Dad sometimes left me in the care of Jim and Rose, sensible children, even at only twelve and eleven. My parents would go out for a drive and sometimes stop for a pint at The Green Dragon at Sambourne or The Neville Arms on the Inkberrow turning.

On the Christmas of 1946 we had a huge tree decorated traditionally with tiny, red, twisted candles and lanterns cunningly made from the foil from inside cigarette packets. We had sparkling lamenta too, dripping like frost and a fairy on top dressed in an outfit made by Auntie Chris from net curtains and tinsel. Someone brought a camera when they visited and the photo shows me in my velvet dressing gown made out of scraps by Dad, looking up at the wonderful tree. In another photo Mum holds me up to reach for an ornament. She looked beautiful with her long wavy hair gripped back and a diamante brooch, bought by Jimmy, pinned to the lapel of her long sleeved winter frock.

I used to trail all around the big house following Mum and Dad, and Daddy decided I should have a chair of my very own to rest on. He would make it himself and, ever resourceful, decided to wander down the road to get a piece of wood from the carpentry shop attached to the undertaker's. He came home very satisfied with an elm off-cut from a coffin lid. This sturdy low chair with oak legs and back rail has stood the test of time and is still admired.

During my early years Dad had been doing electrical wiring and repairs and was doing quite well. He had a partner who didn't pull his weight much, but despite this they decided to open a shop in Bidford on Avon. However, the relative affluence was short lived. Mum was worried that the shop was expanding too quickly, and so it proved. There was considerable competition from similar shops, people were slow to pay for work done, and Dad's partner drew his pay and often did not show up. The business went bust and Dad had to turn his hand to anything that would earn him a few quid.

Mum was expecting another baby and Stephen was born in March 1948. Mum says they were very hard up. She craved a cold drink after Steve was born but could not afford a bottle of squash.

Dad had a struggle to pay the rent of £2.10.00 and then in November 1948 the lease, which had already been extended by a year, to six years, was up and we had to leave.

Chapter 2

∽ Homeless ∽

This part of the story starts in November 1948 when I was just turned four years old and my brother Stephen was just a few months old. Our family house, which Mum and Dad loved, was just starting to look nice. They'd been picking up bits of odd furniture here and there and lavishing care on it. There was not much that Dad couldn't do, or wouldn't have a go at. He would mend broken joints, refit chair arms or table legs, stain and varnish. Between them they would upholster furniture, and Mum, always a superb housekeeper would complete the job with polish and hard work. My parents accepted surplus furniture from the family and rescued chairs that were destined either for the bonfire or to be chopped up for firewood. Mum has got a good eye for colour and style and had our home looking beautiful.

However there was a problem; the house was rented and the six year lease was up. The landlord would not renew it; he wanted to sell the property. My parents were in dire straits. The strain of caring for four children on next to no money was beginning to tell.

Mum tells the story of how Dad's mother, Grandma Ancell was contacted and Auntie Stella and Uncle David who lived with Gran agreed that we could go there as a temporary measure. It would be a tight squeeze. There was Gran, Auntie and Uncle and my three cousins, Wendy, Christopher and Barry. Also they had found room for a lodger, Betty, who was an old friend of Grandma.

Mum and Dad must have wondered where on earth we would fit in. They sold some of our furniture for £45 to give them some ready cash, and our old landlord agreed to store the rest in one of the rooms in the house. All we took with us were our clothes, our bed linen and Steve's cot. Mum and Dad somehow packed it into the car, an old Jaguar, leaving room for three children to squeeze in the back, with Steve on Mum's lap in the front.

Our destination was Hastings in Sussex and Mum says it took twelve hours to limp down there, via Stratford upon Avon, Oxford and High Wycombe. We approached London down Western Avenue and were all tired and irritable by then. We had a puncture and Dad had to change the wheel by the side of the road. We'd played all sorts of games on the long and squashed journey, and Mum had looked out of the car window for things to interest us on the way. As we had got closer to London we had seen field after field of horses and wondered where they had come from. They were huddled up in the corners of fields and looked very dejected. Just like us.

There was a bit more to look at after this. I did not know it then, but the route through London would become etched on my memory with all the journeys we would make to and fro. Bayswater Road to Marble Arch, turn right and down Park Row, round Hyde Park Corner and down through Victoria. We crossed the River Thames by Vauxhall Bridge and passed The Oval cricket ground.

Over a hundred miles gone and less than eighty to go, my parents must have been thinking. On we struggled, the car straining every mile, overheating and having to cool down when we had toilet stops. Sevenoaks, Tonbridge, Robertsbridge, nearly there. Mum and Dad were glad to see Hastings on the signposts now. Finally we arrived and I think it was so traumatic that Mum has erased it from her mind, because she can give me no details of the first few hours following our arrival.

I shared a room with Wendy, then aged seven, and was not allowed to touch anything in her room. Mum, Dad and Stephen shared another room, and Jimmy and Rosemary fitted in somewhere else. Grandma and her friend Betty went to Ireland for a month, maybe just to ease the strain but it certainly must have helped with the allocation of beds!

However, our relief was short lived. Just as we'd left Astwood Bank Jimmy had brought back a mumps infection, and Mum got the illness. Whether or not Steve caught it I'm not sure, but Mum says he was a miserable baby, always blarting – and no wonder, with all the upheaval and tension. This, combined with the fact that Mum was feeling low and finding it difficult to cope made a tense situation. Steve cried most of the night, and when put out in the garden to sleep in his pram, cried most of the time then, too. The small garden backed onto Hastings railway station and only an overgrown alley separated the garden from a very busy marshalling yard with steam whistles and clunking, shunting trains. Sometimes Mum would wheel the pram into the Linton Gardens to get a bit of peace and hope the noisy baby would be lulled off.

We were told that we upset the bathroom routine, which must have been under strain anyway, and Mum could never choose the right moment to wash the nappies or do the family laundry. The neighbours complained about the noise. Grandma Ancell and Auntie Stella had taken enough. We had not been there two weeks but they asked Mum and Dad to leave. It took them another two weeks to find somewhere to go; or rather, someone prepared to find a home for two adults and four children aged six months to fourteen years.

Uncle Peter and Auntie Elsie came to the rescue. This was Dad's brother and Yorkshire born wife, and they had three or four children by then. However, since Uncle had sold his house, the one Gran had given him a deposit for in 1945, he had gone on to a bigger and better house. They said we could move in for a while. Dad had managed to find some casual work by then. One of his jobs was painting a shop and doing the sign writing in the Old Town district of Hastings. He'd had no training in sign writing and dare not burn the original off with the blow lamp, but had to use the outline of the old lettering to guide him.

He also managed to get some work in a line he did know something about: electrical and radio repair. During this time Mum was surprised to get a telephone call one day, from Astwood Bank. Our old house had been sold, the new people had moved in and they wanted our furniture moved out of their sitting room. Mum and Dad had no spare money. What could they do? Mum's older sister Auntie Daye, who lived in Alcester not far from Astwood Bank offered to organise it. She paid £25 for carriage, and the removers Hunt's of Studley brought it down to Hastings, where it had to be put in store.

By then Mum decided she'd had enough, and was ready for a break. She negotiated with the removers and secured a lift for herself, me and Steve back up country to stay with her parents in Alcester for a while, leaving Dad, Jim and Rosemary in Sussex.

While we were away Dad got himself a proper job. It was at the gypsum mines at Mountfield near Netherfield about ten miles inland. It was a long way to go to work but he gave a lift to some other men and they paid towards the petrol.

Needless to say Mum and Dad hated to be apart and Dad knew he had got to do something to persuade Mum back down to Sussex. He secured some rooms in a big old house called The Towers, and we moved back.

Here we all were then, in the spring of 1949, Dad, Mum and the four children. Jimmy aged fourteen and growing fast, Rosemary aged thirteen, me at four years old and Steve almost twelve months old. Jean by now had progressed to the East Sussex Hospital that year to begin her training as a State Registered Nurse.

The Towers was a grand house with huge bay windows with French windows onto the lawn, its louvred shutters and first floor balconies, and its turrets and towers. It was in the Old Town part of Hasting, up at the top of High Street then on up Harold Road. It was owned by a lady in her mid-seventies called Mrs. Whittaker-Swinton, who consoled herself with gin since her daughter had 'run off'. The rent was fixed at £40 a quarter year, and we had quite a bit of space.

The basement contained our kitchen as well as a big hall where bikes could be stored. Leading up from here were six carpeted stairs to the tiled ground floor hall with a beautiful stained glass window. The lounge led off and was well lit by a huge three-bay window down to floor level. The wide stone step which led from the French window down to the lawn was a favourite place to pose for family photographs.

Just two steps up from the hall were the toilet and bathroom. A visit to the toilet was something of an adventure. Uncomfortably elevated on a thick mahogany seat, about four feet wide, and poised over a huge flower-decorated porcelain pan, I can still remember feeling very vulnerable. To flush the toilet one had to pull upwards on a brass handle set within a hemisphere cut out of the wood, and this slid open the door in the bottom of the pan to correspond with a huge deluge of water from the hidden cistern.

The sleeping arrangements were quite civilised. Mum and Dad had a big bedroom with space for Stephen's cot and leading off the lounge through double inter-connecting doors was the room where Rosemary and I slept. Jim did not have a room of his own but the landing was so enormous that a curtain was rigged up across it and he had his bed there.

I have memories of walking down the gracious staircase with wide, shallow steps, the thick carpet held down with brass stair rods. The house had a particular smell: a combination of cabbage and the paraffin oil used to fuel the heating stoves. My parents had a real struggle to find the rent which worked out at three guineas a week, and had to rely on Grandma Ancell helping them out sometimes.

We lived there about eighteen months and during this time I had an accident which had a permanent effect. One day I was running across the lawn, which our landlady proudly described as Cumberland Turf. I was chasing a ball and I tripped over, landing in the rockery. I fell with such force that all my front teeth were pushed into my gums and blood was pouring out of my mouth. Dad and Mum bundled me into the car with a towel against my mouth and set off to try and find a dentist. After driving all round Hastings they finally found one who would look at my injury. My teeth were positioned into some sort of shape, the dentist insisting that they must not come out as it would have a detrimental effect on my adult teeth when they were ready to emerge. His care was not entirely justified as my teeth have never lined up properly to this day.

Another trauma of 1949 was staying in the East Sussex Hospital to have my tonsils out. It seemed to be a menu of jelly every day to ease my sore throat. Whenever she could, Jean, who was nursing there, came to visit me and bring me a picture book.

In May 1949 I was five and began to attend Clive Vale School where Jimmy and Rosemary were already pupils. My first day was not a happy one as someone pushed me in a puddle and I sat in a wet gymslip all afternoon. However I soon settled in and was invited to join in the skipping games.

Dad was Head Electrician at the gypsum mines by then but we still struggled for money. We were all growing at an alarming pace and had to have new school uniforms. We often had visitors at The Towers. Granny Winnett, Auntie Daye and Auntie Chris would come down and Mum and Dad hated to stint on the hospitality. They gradually fell behind with the rent and in the autumn of 1950 we had to leave.

We were offered a couple of rooms at Uncle Peter and Auntie Elsie's again. By this time Uncle had bought a mobile chip lorry and Dad, when he had finished work in the evenings, went out on the round working for his brother to supplement his pay packet, selling fish and chips. The chips were sold for two pennies a portion and I remember seeing Dad chipping up the potatoes, forcing the spuds one by one through a hand-operated chip

Granny and Grandad Winnett in their garden, Alcester 1952.

cutter. A short while after this Uncle Peter sold up and moved his family up to Whitehaven.

Despite being two years old Steve still cried a lot. Mum often used to get up at 5 a.m. to try and pacify him so he would not wake the whole household. It was all a great strain and Mum was at a very low ebb. Everyone grumbled about Stephen and because of this Mum developed a very special relationship with him, wanting to protect him from being the subject of everyone's complaints. This special love did not, alas, stop him crying and we were soon asked to leave Uncle's.

Dad knew a work mate up the North Road in Hastings and he offered us a room on the understanding that the two eldest, Jim and Rose, could not be accommodated. They had to go and live with Gran and Auntie Stella and we moved into our new digs. Mum tells me it was absolutely awful. I had to sleep in the double bed with her and Dad, and Steve's cot was jammed in at the bottom of the bed. Needless to say they could not stand it and after a few weeks decided to leave.

There was only one option left and Mum asked her mother if she could take me and Steve up to Alcester to live. I left my infant school and Dad drove us up to Gran's house just after Christmas. It was two and a half years since we left our home in Astwood Bank and this was my seventh move. Once he had delivered us Dad had to drive back to Hastings and move in with Jim and Rose living with his mother and sister in Braybrooke Road.

While living with Granny I had to sleep in the double bed between her and Grandad. I can remember being woken at night by the sound of Grandad using the chamber pot which he had pulled out from under the bed.

Auntie Chris, who was not married, lived at home with Granny and Grandad. She had a very nice bedroom with a high, single bed and a dressing table decorated with pink crocheted doilies upon which stood glass powder bowls, candle sticks and her brush, comb and mirror. Her oak bookcase was crammed with novels published by The Book Club.

Auntie lavished attention on me, and made me new clothes and knitted me a cardigan depicting Rupert Bear on each side of the front buttons. My fair hair was parted in the middle, plaited and tied with satin bows. Having no children of her own, Auntie Chris loved doing this. I often wore a gingham dress with a smocked bodice, puff sleeves and a white collar. Photographs show that when the weather was hot I either wore just my knickers or a woolly-looking swim suit for playing in Granny's garden. I had an old dolly with a sort of pottery head. I loved her to bits and Auntie Chris made many sets of clothes for her.

Mum and Steve slept in Auntie Daye's room as she worked away from home during the week. At the weekends they had to double up in the bed. Mum was glad to be with her mother for a while and it seemed like a sanctuary after all the upheaval of the previous couple of years. Dad used to send money up when he could afford to, but of course he had to pay for himself, Jim and Rose.

Grandad was a man with a short fuse, and expected the household to revolve round his needs. He demanded peace and quiet, and believed children could be seen but not heard. Steve was getting quite boisterous and he had always been noisy, so this made Mum's life rather difficult. She had to put Steve in his pushchair and take him up the back fields, out of sight and sound, and come back when Grandad had calmed down. Sometimes he would go up to The Roebuck for a pint and then we could all relax for a while.

Grandad was a tall, gangly man and his tweed sports jacket, patched on the elbows with leather off-cuts, hung from his thin shoulders. When he stood straight he looked an imposing figure. A scowl would often crease his high, chestnut-coloured forehead and he could freeze you to the spot with a piercing glare from his cold blue eyes. His moustache seemed to bristle with anger and Steve and I were terrified of him.

The house was built by the council between the wars, and like many of that era had a big garden, in fact, it was bigger than the others as the house was on a corner plot. It was situated at the end of a cul-de-sac which led off the main Birmingham Road in Alcester. A lane led round the end separating it from an ancient barn, farm house and mill which was the mill for Ragley Hall some miles away in the village of Arrow. Granny used to get her eggs from John the farmer and Auntie Chris would hold my hand and lead me across the farmyard guiding me past ducks, geese, guinea fowl and chickens.

Further round the bend, along the lane and past some rented out garages Mr. Godfrey kept his pig. It had a brick built sty and run, and along one wall a huge, glazed clay, half-drainpipe was cemented into place as a trough. Mr. Godfrey would boil the pig swill in an old copper boiler he had erected on site. The sticks underneath it soon kindled into a blaze which kept going until all the scraps bubbled into a thick broth. Like many of the local people Granny kept a pig bucket for kitchen scraps and also saved stale bread for the chickens, when it was not needed for a bread pudding.

The lane ran alongside the backs of the long gardens of the houses in Birmingham Road and from there on became a grassy path which led up the back fields. It was lovely: the mill race was diverted from the River Arrow and was controlled by sluice gates before it reached the now defunct mill wheel. The river itself moved quite quickly and had undercut the bank on one side leaving a shingly beach on the other side. This walk was a favourite one for Mum to take me and Steve to paddle.

Meanwhile I had started to attend the infants' school, and loved the walk down the main road past the Grammar School, and past the almshouses where Great Granny Winnett lived. Gran referred to her as 'The Old Lady'. She was not a blood relative but was in the unusual position of being stepmother to both my grandmother and grandfather, but of course, I did not know this strange strand of our family history at that time. Just after this terrace of eight houses was the cemetery with its oak lych-gate and gravel paths. Several of my relatives were buried here, and Granny would recite the dates of their births and deaths. We then turned the left corner down School

Road and finally reached the school set back in its playground. I did not attend this school for long but remember making a Humpty Dumpty on a wall out of an eggshell glued onto a match box, painted to represent bricks.

Sometimes Granny would meet me, wearing her white-spotted blue frock which matched the colour of her eyes. Her square, ruby-glass brooch would glint at the neck.

'Would you like to go to Mr. Everett's for an ice cream?' she would ask.

'Yes please, a pink one', I excitedly replied. Granny would hold my hand and lead me across the road, up another lane past the tennis courts and up an alley into Priory Road. Mr. Everett's shop was up two steps, and I entered the shop which was filled with jars of every sort of sweet imaginable as well as a refrigerator containing the tubs of ice cream.

Occasionally, after school we might walk up the road towards Arrow and look at the elephant tree. This enormous tree was set high on a bank and its gnarled and exposed roots looked just like an elephant with four legs, head and trunk.

One afternoon a week we would call to see the Old Lady. Granny would lead me round the back of the almshouses and we entered by the back door. Great-granny Winnett would often be lying on her plush-covered day-bed and expected her step-daughter to make the tea. Granny would open the huge brass-bound mahogany coal box and take out a couple of lumps of coal with the tongs. The old lady resented this but knew if she wanted a cup of tea the fire must be stoked up. Granny would reach over the brass-topped, high fireguard and plant the kettle on the trivet that was wedged on the bars of the high grate. Then she would stretch up to the mantelpiece which was covered with a velvet cloth with dangly, dusty bobbles all along the edge. She would lift down the japanned tea-caddy and put it ready next to the pot. I would be positioned on the high dark-oak stool with its carpet covered top held down by brass domed upholstery tacks. After we had all sipped our tea Granny would carry the cups over to the shallow, brown crock sink and swill them off. She would pour any remaining hot water into a crock hot water bottle and pass it to her complaining step-mother and it was time for me to kiss the whiskery cheek and say goodbye, without dislodging the aspidistra from its tall bamboo stand. As I moved closer the old lady seemed to rustle as her scarves and shawls moved across her layers of black clothing, and she extended a claw-like hand from a lace-fringed cuff, not with a hoped-for sixpence but to grasp my wrist and bid me visit her again. Great-granny's frail and wizened body would flop back against the arm of her day-bed and we would escape into the sunlight.

Sometimes at weekends Granny would take me to see Aunt Sarah, one of her sisters and three years younger than Granny. She lived at what Granny called The Workhouse but for many years it had been the geriatric hospital, 'Oversley House'. Aunt Sarah knitted me a scarf once, but had run out of wool before it was completed and it was only about eighteen inches long and barely long enough to go once round my neck.

Another outing I looked forward to was to go with Auntie Chris, who was one of the leading lights of the ladies tennis team, to the courts on Sunday morning. I sat on the grass and watched her play a few games with her special friend and life long companion Bert Taylor. Auntie Chris was tall, like all the Winnetts and shared their long straight nose and blue eyes. Her pretty blonde hair was regularly waved and she enhanced her eye colour with soft blue eye-shadow. Her arms and legs glowed with a healthy tan and her tennis shorts and blouse set off her lithe figure.

Granny had spent most of her life in Alcester and knew many people. Her special friends were Mr. and Mrs. Spooner who lived a couple of doors away, and Mr. and Mrs. Handy who lived round the back. Cora Johnson would visit regularly on her bike having cycled down from her house just over the hump-backed railway bridge on the road to Alcester Heath. Gran shopped in all the shops that had been in Alcester for years and had her hair done in Mr. Keyte's salon. She would emerge from the hairdresser looking pinkly self-conscious, her hair in tight, permed curls. With her fortnightly hair-do all she had to do to maintain it was crimp it nightly into stiff, wave-like peaks with sprung, metal waving clips.

She mainly patronized the Alcester Co-operative Society, and looked forward to the dividend payout each year. On visits to the drapery department I would sit on the high bentwood chair provided for customers and watch as shallow mahogany drawers were slid carefully out from beneath the glass-topped counter. They might contain vests or knickers, nightgowns or stockings. Having selected what she wanted, Granny would quote her dividend number and hand over her cash. The assistant placed it together with a little chitty in a brass cylinder. This was inserted in a tube and "whoosh" as if by magic it shot across the room into the cash office in the corner. Here, protected by sheet glass and resting on a thick wooden counter the clerk would enter the purchase and return the change by the same shuttle.

I loved my outings with Granny Winnett and felt proud and reassured to hold her hand and trot along beside her as she swept majestically down the street. Gran was tall, about five feet nine inches, and stood strong and proud. To me her hair always was grey and her kind face would readily crease into a smile, crinkling the corners of her sapphire eyes. I now know that she had a lot of hardships to endure in her life but she never appeared short tempered, except perhaps, when Grandad tried her sorely. For me she would bathe cut knees, soothe ant bites, gently comb knotted hair and unravel my knitting wool.

Mum was not happy in Alcester for long. Both her sisters were fed up with not being able to use the bathroom as Mum needed to do the laundry and bath us children. She missed Dad and dropped in weight to under eight stone.

She would write to Dad regularly and one day in February 1951 she told him that Steve had called Grandad "Daddy". This maddened Dad and he sent word to say he would be driving up on Sunday to collect us all. He did not want his son not to know its father.

Dad had organised us some digs with a work mate of his, Frank Millett. They lived in a tall ramshackle house with a basement but nevertheless it was crowded and a real muddle. Frank and Elsie had two children, Clifford and Christine, who each had their own room. Mum and Dad had a small room together but there was no room for Steve and me. We had to cram in with Frank and Elsie whose bigger room was next door on the same landing.

All this time Dad had worked at the gypsum mines which had expanded with a vastly increased workforce. The council had decided to build a new estate, mainly for these employees, at Darvell Down about a mile from the mines. Building work was in progress and our new house had been promised for the past two months. Mum and Dad were so looking forward to a house of their own, but it was a long time coming.

One Friday evening while Mum and Elsie sat at home canking together with us four children, Dad was very late home. He eventually arrived with a wonderful surprise. He had the key for our new home. Long-suffering but dispirited, Dad had finally realised that actions speak louder than words. He'd been to the council offices at Battle to demand the key. When they had threatened closure Dad said he'd sit on the doorstep until he got a key. Finally they issued one. Mum was ecstatic. She asked Elsie to look after me and Steve and she and Dad went and camped out in their new home, number fifty-one, that very night.

During all the recent moves for Dad, Mum and us younger children, Jim and Rosemary had been lodging with Grandma Ancell in Hastings. They were both due to leave school and moved up to Netherfield with us and started work. Rose secured a job in a dress shop in Hastings and commuted daily by bus. Jim worked in the office at the gypsum mines and was able to walk there by the track across the fields. After about a year, when Jim was seventeen he decided to join the Royal Navy and went as a cadet to HMS Chatham to begin his training.

Our time at Darvell Down was happy despite the demanding work in the mine for Dad and the pressure of a big family for Mum. We had a dog and a nice garden to play in. Dad built us a log cabin with a veranda and Steve and I, together with our friends, spent many happy hours pretending it was a Wild West stockade, a castle or a lowly house.

The Milletts had moved to their new house at Darvell Down about the same time as us, and I shared my childhood fantasies with Christine. We used to run free in the woods that led to the gypsum mines, climbing trees and making dens.

The housing estate was eventually finished and proper roads were laid. They were made of concrete with each long piece joined to the next with black pitch. We watched while it melted in huge iron vats with a scorching flame underneath and then was poured into the slots from buckets tilted by blue-overalled roadmen.

I attended the village school at Netherfield and on my seventh birthday in May 1951 we had a class photo taken. As a special privilege I was allowed to sit right at the centre front on a woven-rush gym mat. The walk to school seemed a long one. Up from the estate on to the top road; turn left along the ridge then fork left down a narrow lane to the school. It was probably only about a mile but was fraught with dangers, real and imaginary. Along the edge of this lane there was a spinney and winding through the beech trees was a mossy path. It had the local name of Mary Anne's Wood and was supposedly haunted. With the wind moaning and the leaves rustling we'd scare ourselves witless with fears of being pursued by Mary Anne.

Back in the Midlands, with Auntie Daye working in the office of the Austin Motor Company in Longbridge and Auntie Chris in the office of The

High Duty Alloys aluminium casting plant in Redditch, which opened in 1939 to make, amongst other things, aircraft parts, all the news was of people prospering. The Midlands was where the money was, everyone said. This, combined with Mum missing her mother's support and caring love, helped the decision that we would try to move back to that area. With Auntie Chris's help sending back information, Dad secured a job as a maintenance electrician at the HDA in February 1952, and moved back in with Granny, Grandad and Auntie Chris once again.

He put our name on the list for a council house in Redditch and hoped it would not be too long before we were allocated a house. Poor Mum and Dad must have wondered if they would ever have a stable family life again and I believe that it was only their deep affection for each other that kept them going through these bad times. As for myself, looking back over these early years of my life, I think that these experiences helped to make me resourceful and resilient and gave me the confidence to face up to whatever life threw at me, and to see the best in situations.

Mum had Elsie for a friend but missed Dad very much. They adored each other but had endured very difficult times since leaving Astwood Bank in 1948. Dad sent back money for us, and sometimes if she could afford it Mum would leave Rosemary, then just seventeen, to look after Stephen and me while she visited Dad for the weekend.

Dad kept pestering the council for a house and one day noticed a big, run down, detached house that was empty. It had been used as a hostel in the war and was in a very dilapidated state. He managed to secure a viewing of the house and told the council he would be willing to take it on if the rent was right. It was finally agreed and in September 1952 Mum, Dad, Rosemary, Stephen and I all moved into our house in South Street, Redditch.

The Exodus was over.

Chapter 3

∽ Fitting in ∾

The house that became our first long term family home since 1948 was a daunting prospect. Neglect manifested itself in the usual ways: a dampish, unoccupied smell, chipped paintwork and grubby walls. All over the house the floorboards were covered with thick brown lino. The electrical wiring looked ancient and positively dangerous, the plumbing system was Dickensian.

'I've had a go at the toilet and bath already,' Dad informed Mum. 'You would have run a mile if you'd seen it before.'

Mum looked disbelievingly into the toilet bowl and left the bathroom before being contaminated.

The task ahead was formidable but my parents were never a couple to flinch from hard work. With their combination of style and skill they set about turning this sad house into a wonderful home. Never did they let the fact that it was a 'council house' albeit an unconventional one, stand in the way of making alterations to house and garden or spending their money on creating a beautiful haven.

This was to be our home for twenty years and holds indelible memories of childhood. The house was in South Street, off a turning at the bottom of Mount Pleasant. The street was a hill; the top half more gentle and the bottom half, after it was bisected by West Street and West Avenue, was very steep.

Most of the houses were in late nineteenth century terraces, some with tiny front gardens and some directly edged the pavement. However, on one side of the top section of the road there was an impressively large house called 'Oldcrest', with a wide gate and a drive. Lime trees bordered the entranceway and hung over the fence leaving the pavement in dappled shade. Below this house were three other detached houses, numbers forty three, forty five and forty seven. Ours was the middle one and basked in the reflected glory of Oldcrest. They had all been used as hostels in the war and Oldcrest was the local YWCA and remained in municipal use as a school dental surgery and training centre, I believe.

Our house sat four-square and double fronted. There was a square bay window to the left of the front door and an angled bay to the right. A tiled porch resting on a substantial post protected the front door. There was a side passage to a high, solid gate which gave access to the rear garden and back door.

The garden seemed huge and was very overgrown. At the bottom of the slope were two old gnarled apple trees and rusty iron railings. The other side of this was a wilderness, a completely unkempt area of trees with ash, hawthorn, the odd plum and a huge balsam poplar tree, which cast its sticky catkins each spring.

The back yard had three interesting doors opening from it. On that first day we unlatched them in turn. A toilet with a huge stained bowl and rusty chain, a long store shed full of junk and coal dust and another outbuilding with a small fireplace and chimney which Dad immediately earmarked as his workshop. On the other side of the yard loomed a solid looking flat-roofed building with doorways framed by huge concrete blocks. About four feet away from these openings was a thick brick wall the same height as the building. Dad said it was an air-raid shelter and that we would soon have it cleared out. It became an invaluable store room for garden tools and mowers, bicycles and car bits. The other side of the central division was the fuel store with the remains of a heap of coke.

There was still the house to explore and during the first week we familiarised ourselves with its layout and nooks and crannies.

The hall bisected the house from front door to back, and under the lino we found a multi-coloured tiled floor. It was soon cleaned up and polished to show off its lozenges, squares and triangles, gleaming up in blues and whites, greens, reds and browns.

The two front rooms were almost the same size but the slightly smaller one was designated the living room, and the other one, the best lounge. Passing the staircase with turned banisters you faced the back door with two panes of bubbly glass and this led to the back porch. If you turned right you were in the dining room and on the left was the kitchen.

The kitchen was dominated by the fireplace with a high mantle-shelf and crouching on the slabs was a huge stove. This bulbous contraption was covered in knobs and handles which operated various dampers or facilitated refuelling with coke and lower down riddled the ashes. It was painted silver and slivers of aluminium paint floated off onto the tiles. Each side of the chimney breast were alcove cupboards which always remained inconvenient as you had to move chairs to open the doors.

That was not the only inconvenience. As you entered the kitchen from the hall the great, deep, Belfast crock sink was right inside the door. Anyone standing at the sink would get their hip bashed as people pushed the door open. The pantry was almost half the size of the kitchen and had a perforated zinc window covering, a narrow slate shelf under the window and a huge marble shelf beside a deep cupboard. The quarry tiled floor was filthy and spiders must have trapped generations of flies in dozens of cobwebs.

Upstairs were three bedrooms, a huge bathroom and a tiny box room. So, we started a new chapter of our life: the Claysmith family in South Street.

We soon got to meet the neighbours. On one side were the Huin family whose daughter Jane became a friend. On the other side were the Nicholls whose son Christopher became a friend, and sometimes a scapegoat for my brother. Fifty years on we are still close friends with Fred and Christine Nicholls.

I was enrolled at St. Luke's Church of England controlled school and began my schooling there in class 2A, aged eight years and four months. The school was in Rectory Road, Headless Cross and seemed a very long walk although it was only half a mile or so. After the first week I recognised a class mate who also walked up Mount Pleasant. We became companions and very quickly were close friends and inseparable all through our childhood and young adulthood. Her name was Sylvia and I was soon drawn into the warmth of her family as we shared everything.

Starting a new school was no great trauma for me. I had already been to three. I was allocated a team which were named after ranges of local hills. Mine was Malvern and I wore a yellow sash for P.E. and games. I settled down to enjoy school life and to have the fun that now seems a thousand years away looking back over just over fifty years.

So, each morning I would turn left up Mount Pleasant and pass the little rank of shops; a café, Mrs. Laighty's, Mrs. Stanley's greengrocery, and Mrs. Chatterley's the confectioner and tobacconist.

I would walk on up to where the Council House occupied a corner site. Here I would look out for Sylvia who would time her departure to reach the

Me, 1952 Class 2A Headless Cross Junior School.

main road to coincide with me passing by. She lived in Oakly Road, about the same distance from Mount Pleasant as me but on the western side. In a few more months Sylv's house would be like a second home to me as I became accepted as an extra family member.

We would greet each other and fall into step, sometimes linking arms to show the world what close friends we were. We would pass Ivor Road steeply off to the right, then Mount Pleasant post office and the top of Mayfields Estate. Further on, opposite the Park Inn we turned right into Rectory Road and the school playground.

School was wonderful and the work did not seem a great challenge. I liked English and Geography, Art and Nature study. We had a school garden with a pond and used to spend a couple of lessons a week, weeding, sowing seeds and looking at insects and frog spawn and the other wonders of nature.

Like all school children then, we had a bottle of milk each day: one third of a pint, and all the bottles were left in huge crates in the school playground. By the time the milk monitors for each class had heaved them in at mid-morning break the milk had often started to turn sour and we could not stomach it. In winter it would freeze solid and the plug of ice would force up the cardboard lid from the bottle.

I stayed for school dinners, it was too far to walk back home. We paid our dinner money on Monday after the register was called. This was followed by 'savings'. Everyone who could afford it brought sixpence and bought a savings stamp to lick and glue into their books. When the books were full, forty weeks later, near the end of the school year, we could either claim our £1 or deposit it in the Post Office Savings Bank.

School dinners were eaten in the dinner hall on the other side of the road, on the infant school site. We crossed the road in a crocodile, the girls holding hands with a friend, the boys pushing each other out of line. Trestle tables topped with marble patterned lino were set up with a long wooden form down each side and we sat eight to a table to eat a very nice dinner for one shilling (ten pence).

I hated P.E. and games. I was inclined to plumpness and never felt my best exposed in my bottle-green gym knickers with their long legs and elastic which cut into my thighs. Whenever possible we had gym in the playground where we did our exercises on individual oval coconut mats, and learnt a dozen ways to stretch using coloured hula-hoops. Skipping was hateful. I usually missed my run-in and got tangled in the rope, and even if I did get in alright I did not enjoy jumping up and down. I much preferred to play hopscotch after school. We would draw a pattern on the pavement with chalk, sometimes a snail and sometimes squares and triangles. I could throw my stone accurately into the right square and hop from number to number.

During my early years at this school it was discovered during a school medical that I had a curvature of the spine. Not serious, but in those days deportment was everything and a straight back was the key to success. Standing sideways my spine curved in too much at the waist and out too much by my shoulders. My head stuck forward, or so they said, and my top vertebrae formed a prominent lump. The school doctors in their wisdom decided that physiotherapy would cure it.

So on two afternoons a week I was excused the last hour of school and left at 3 o'clock. I walked down Mount Pleasant but instead of turning down Beaufort Street when I got to the Plough and Harrow pub I carried on down front hill, along Evesham Street and crossing by the traffic lights, walked down the Parade. I turned the corner by The Redditch Building Society into Church Road, and then I walked down as far as the Gaumont and turned up a gravelly track beside the bus depot. On the right hand side were a couple of wooden huts which formed the physiotherapy department of the Smallwood Hospital.

For about forty five minutes I had to strip off (again) and with various other youngsters with similar odd problems had to do exercises that involved flattening the small of my back against the floor. What with the long walk, getting on for two miles I should think, and the humiliation of sporting my liberty bodice and knickers, I would rather have been at school. And my back still is not cured!

Meanwhile, things were moving on for the rest of the family.

Jean had finished her State Registered Nurse training at the Royal East Sussex hospital and was working as a qualified nurse. Not for long though. She felt she had chosen the wrong career and soon decided to enrol at the Bishop Otter teacher training college.

Jim had entered the Royal Navy as a cadet and passed out from Chatham as a radio operator and sported a "sparks" badge on his sleeve. I remember him coming home on leave, navy blue bell-bottom sailors' trousers and itchy wool jumper, immaculate, still showing accurate folds, carefully preserved by slipping the garments under his mattress at night. His crisp white collar edged with blue and the blancoed lanyard and spats completed the uniform. He went on to become a Leading Seaman then a deputy Petty Officer. I loved receiving postcards from around the world and particularly treasured the Spanish ones depicting a flamenco dancer with her bright frock embroidered in thick strands of silk.

Rosemary had secured a job in Turner's drapery shop in Alcester Street once we had all moved to Redditch. She stayed there until early 1954 and then moved to the wages office of Terry's, the famous spring manufacturers.

Mum had started a part time job once Steve began school in 1953 and worked as a cashier in a factory canteen. She was always home by the time we arrived back from school, waiting with a snack.

Dad was still working for H.D.A. doing the long shifts that were essential to enhance his pay packet. My parents were making improvements to our home all the time. There was always furniture being mended and joints re-glued. Dad made a window seat in the lounge bay window and Mum sewed cushions for the top and a gathered skirt for the front. Another huge woodwork project was the building of an oak refectory table and matching bench. These were stained and varnished and looked wonderful when the dining room was reorganised. An oak blanket box followed, the lid being fabricated from the leaf of a wonky antique dining table previously owned by Great Granny Winnett. Mum upholstered stools and chairs and made cushions.

Mum was quite innovative with her interiors and would choose delightful wallpaper and co-ordinating curtain fabric. The lounge was a mellow haven and had been enhanced by a new fireplace which Dad both designed and built out of brickettes, and featured tiled-top seats each side of the hearth. This was so admired he designed a second one, for the living room. This had a curved top with side plinths for a few choice ornaments.

The cavernous bathroom had been updated and was now resplendent with a dazzling wallpaper featuring tropical fish swimming in an azure sea moving in and out of waving seaweeds. The floor was covered in new black and white chequered lino and Dad made new aluminium towel rails.

The bathroom paper had been chosen to reflect Dad's hobby, although it is scarcely believable that he had time for one. His passion was tropical fish and he kept his aquarium on a shelf in the kitchen. Over the years he built up a beautiful collection: black mollies and orange platys, zebras and tiger barbs, graceful angel fish, neon tetras and two-a-penny guppies. Every month Dad would clean out the tank. Steve, who still sat on the draining board with his feet in the sink, to have his knees scrubbed, sometimes spotted a tiny fish trapped in the plug hole, having been accidentally sucked up the siphon tube. Needless to say, Mum did not think it was funny.

I thrived on being a loved and slightly spoilt member of an extended family. My parents worked hard to make up for all the misfortunes we had suffered during the past four years. Dad worked every hour he could at H.D.A., doing a different shift each week. He dreaded leaving for the 10pm-6am shift, kissing Mum goodbye and departing for the eight hour stint as a maintenance electrician. The company forged aluminium parts and some nights you could hear the thump of "The Big Hammer" as it whacked down relentlessly on the sheets of alloy.

Another sound which was more noticeable at night was the train as it went through a tunnel which passed under our house on its way from the station. The glass in the windows would sometimes rattle and if we strained our ears we could hear a change in the engine noise as it left the tunnel near the Mayfields Estate.

The High Duty Alloys Company had an annual Christmas party for employees' children. We would race around the canteen playing musical chairs and pass the parcel. Finally when tired and giddy we would flop into our chairs to eat sandwiches and bright jelly with two slices of cling peaches set in it, served in paper dishes. Once Steve was five he was allowed to come, and I had to look after him. The climax was queuing for our gift from Father Christmas before being driven home.

The Coronation in June 1953 was a spectacular local event. We had a fancy-dress parade and a tea party. Four children from our group of houses entered. I was dressed as a Dutch girl with a very uncomfortable bonnet, Steve was Sir Francis Drake. Chris Nicholls was the Coronation crown and Jane Huin an Elizabethan courtier. Like so many families, this is when we purchased our first television and sat around it to watch the coronation ceremony of Queen Elizabeth II.

Auntie Chris worked in an office, spending many years in the wages department of H.D.A. and some time at the Needle Industries in Studley. During school holidays I would stay at Alcester for a few days. I would meet Auntie off the bus which stopped at the top of the lane and we would walk back to Gran's for tea.

'Please let me tidy out your bucket-bag, Auntie,' I pleaded.

'Alright dear, but tip everything onto a sheet of newspaper first,' she agreed.

Out would spill old sandwich bags, her spectacle case, sunglasses, sometimes some knitting, keys, identity card wallet, pens, diary and purse. What I really hoped for was that there would be some loose change from her bus fare. Rather than put the coins back in her purse she would drop them into the leather open-topped bag. I would make the coins into a little pile at the edge of the newspaper and without fail Auntie Chris would say,

'Keep the change for pocket money.'

She loved knitting and often made a jumper or cardigan for me, ranging from the one with Rupert Bear when I was five, to stylish cable patterns in beautiful colours which I wore in my late teens. When I was about six or seven years old Auntie taught me how to knit. She bought a ball of brightly coloured rainbow wool and some plastic knitting pins and patiently instructed me. These lessons were reinforced by Granny and I soon had the idea. I also learnt corking which involved working on an old empty wooden cotton reel on top of which four tacks had been hammered. By careful looping over of a length of wool which had been woven round the tacks a long tail of interlocking wool would appear through the bottom end of the cotton reel. When you had completed a sufficient length you could neatly stitch it up into shape, forming table mats or even slippers.

Auntie must have been concerned about my hands which were usually cold. When I was about five years old she gave me for a Christmas present, a muff which dangled from a cord which went behind my head and sat under my coat collar. It was lovely to ram my chilly fingers into the fur lined muff. A couple of years later the muff was superseded by a pair of rabbit skin gloves. They were too big for my hands and I had a job to grip things with the leather palms, but Auntie loved it when I stroked the brown flecked fur with a bare hand. When she was going through her creative handicraft phase I would receive a pair of rather shapeless sheepskin mittens each Christmas.

On my birthday I would be treated to a day in Birmingham. For tea we would visit Lewis's restaurant on the top floor of the store. There were linen table cloths and cakes were brought round on a trolley. A band played discreetly at the side but on these special days Auntie Chris would request a tune for me. They usually played Teddy Bears' Picnic and dedicated it to me on my birthday.

Each Saturday at about 5 o'clock the family would drive down to Alcester to visit Granny and Grandad Winnett. We were always expected at the same time but as Steve and I would disrupt the recording of the football results on the coupons I'm not sure why we went then. Grandad would sit close to the radio and turn the volume up. He cussed us if he missed a score or if his pencil broke. Gran would be in the back kitchen making tea and loading into tins the baking she had done for us. To last the week we had a bread pudding in an enamel basin, a jam or apple tart depending on the season and two dozen fairy cakes.

Granny kept her house immaculate. The oak dining table and the sideboard with an oval mirror at the back gleamed with polish. The silver rose bowl, won by Grandad for having the best council house garden for five years running, shimmered in the late afternoon sunlight. The grandfather clock ticked regularly, and seemed to keep in time with the 1930s mantelpiece clock. The kettle and trivet in the hearth, the brass shell case and the ashtrays on the windowsill had all been well rubbed with metal polish and glowed warmly.

Sometimes Mum would take a bottle of beer for Grandad and a Guinness for Granny, but best of all they would love an evening drive out to a country pub where they could have a round of drinks while Steve and I sat in the pub garden with our Smiths' crisps and glasses of orangeade.

A visit to Granny's house would sometimes hold other excitements. If Grandad had been out beating for the shoot he might have been given a pheasant, or he may have shot a rabbit, up the back fields. They would hang for a couple of days in the cupboard under the stairs and I would be allowed, with morbid fascination, to open the door and inspect them. The gas meter was also housed in this cupboard and I would be lifted up to feed it with big copper pennies to keep the supply going.

Although Auntie Chris lived with my grandparents she was not always there when we visited. She had a busy social life and enjoyed playing tennis, flower arranging and going out with Uncle Bert, her lifelong companion. They would drive into the countryside and take Bert's cocker spaniel, Sherry, for a walk, and maybe stop off at a country pub for a drink.

At last we could start to put the past traumas behind us. My parents had picked themselves up, dusted themselves off, and started all over again. Their hopes were coming to fruition, and things were stabilizing. I had fitted into this new chapter of family history and my place was secure.

Chapter 4

❧ Bibles, ballet and bonding ❧

My life, when not involved in school or family outings, revolved around the church. Sylvia, her mother and sister all attended Headless Cross Methodist Church, whose open-work spire is such a feature on the main Evesham road. I asked my parents if I could go with my friend to the Sunday school there and they agreed. We met up at our usual place, at the top of Salop Road, and the four of us walked up for Sunday morning service. It was further than school, almost twice the distance, but dressed up in our best frocks and chattering all the way the journey passed quickly.

Everyone had their own favourite pew and we entered via the porch, were greeted and handed a hymn book, and walked along the tiled vestibule to the furthest door, leading to the left aisle. We sat in the centre block, the row where an iron pillar supported the upper balcony.

The children went into the church with everyone else for the first hymn and prayer and then filed out through the side door next to the organ, into the Sunday school room. Once we were in the school room the superintendent took over. The hall seemed huge and had a stage at one end. Around the sides of the room were many doors. About five or six led to smaller classrooms, one led to the Primary schoolroom and one led to the billiard room.

On the walls hung huge pictures, depicting the life of Jesus and the parables. These pictures were in bright colours carefully and perfectly shaded in pencil crayons.

The Sunday school was organised like a day school, with classes according to age in primary and junior departments, each with their individual teacher, and all under the responsibility of the superintendent. We had our own service with a starting hymn then split up into classes for our lesson. We all came together again for a final hymn, carefully timed to finish the same time that the congregation flocked out of church.

This was a very sociable time as everyone wished each other all the best and asked God's blessings and shook hands with each other and the minister. Our minister at the time was the Rev. J. B. Chapman. This interaction was called the fellowship of Methodism and we truly felt we were one big family.

Sylvia's family were close friends with Mr & Mrs. Woods and their son David. I have such wonderful memories of visiting their house, the gardener's cottage at Southcrest. If we arrived early Mrs. Woods would answer the door with floury hands, brushing back strands of hair from her beaming, pinkly warm face. She would be hurrying to get the baking done, and on the tiled hearth in front of the fire would be dough rising in brown mixing bowls covered with damp cloths.

'Turn those round for me dears,' she would request. 'Then set the table, please.'

Once the clearing up was done and the dough risen the loaves would be put in the oven of the Parkray, then the sultana dough cut up and shaped into rounds.

Within the hour we would be sitting down to salad from Mr. Woods' garden and greenhouse, fresh baked bread and buttered hot Yorkshire tea buns.

David remained a staunch friend all through my teenage and college years and I am godmother to his eldest daughter.

In the autumn of 1953 when I was nine, I was enrolled at the School of Dancing run by Miss Elsie Sidelle Downing. Auntie Chris paid the fees and presumably cherished the idea that I might develop into a young lady. I went to classes in ballet, American tap dancing and acrobatics. I did not excel at any of them but quite enjoyed going to the dance studio in Littleworth, off Evesham Street.

I was not a slim child and it was with some effort that I learnt to place my feet in ballet positions from one to five. I felt slightly self conscious when holding the bar in front of the huge mirror. Dad always joked he would carve my bottom or thighs for a nice slice of tasty brisket with a jug of gravy, so it took some nerve to gain the confidence to expose legs like tree trunks.

In February 1954 I took my tap exam in the preparatory grade and passed with 79% but my certificate records that I lacked style and attack. Still, the pleated satin skirt with shoulder straps that went with my co-ordinating blouse was quite nice, and I can still dance some of the routines that I learnt!

Palace Theatre 1954 Miss Elsie Sidelle Downing's ballet pupils. Me, back row, right.

Later on that year I performed in a show at the Palace Theatre in Alcester Street. The ballet involved eleven of us budding young ballerinas and our prima ballerina. I had a yellow tutu with a satin bodice that stretched tightly across my undeveloped chest and podgy stomach. We carried garlands of crepe-paper flowers and cavorted about in front of a backdrop depicting sea-shore and mountains.

The acrobatic show that followed, which I liked least because it involved cartwheels and backbends, splits and handstands, featured about ten of us in pierot's outfits and we looked like so many Andy Pandys with green suits gathered up into red flounced cuffs at our wrists and ankles.

Although I attended dancing classes for a couple of years it was still the church and bible study that provided a pivotal point in my life outside the family.

Around this time in my life, aged about nine, Sylvia and I, along with other Sunday school members, were encouraged to collect money for the Methodist Missionary Society. We had to ask between six and ten people if they would make a commitment to contribute a few pence each week towards "missions at home and overseas".

We had a little card to note down the weekly payments opposite peoples' names. At the end of each year our total was recorded and our certificate updated. These huge certificates were coloured in garish orange and royal blue, and there were spaces to record seven years' collections and pictured children of different nationalities in a circle each year. Alongside the pictures was a space for recording the date and amount and a new coloured seal was glued on annually before the presentation on Missionary Sunday.

I usually managed to collect between twelve and fifteen shillings but in 1956 I excelled myself. I must have found about eight people willing to donate two or three pennies each week because I collected £5 that year and was awarded the missionary society's DSO for Zeal and for God.

Towards the end of this chapter of my life I began attending Bible Study Classes with Sylvia and other Sunday school pupils. We sat an annual scripture exam and received delightful certificates depicting a beautifully illustrated bible story. My album confirms that I must have devoted an evening a week to bible study until I was fourteen and learnt enough of the scriptures to quote passages and answer questions in quite difficult exams.

The Sunday school year culminated in a celebration of the date on which it was founded. Anniversary Day meant best frocks, spotless socks and gloves and no giggling. We sang special hymns for the congregation and received our awards for attendance and scripture exams. The prize books that I received formed the backbone of my childhood reading together with those given me for Christmas and birthday presents. I read of The Magic Faraway Tree, The Famous Five, and The Secret Seven. I escaped to the world of girls' boarding schools and pony-owning families. I travelled with missionaries to foreign climes and with the heroines of the novels forgave and forgot the wrongs done to me.

It was the horse books that eventually got the upper hand, and finally when we were almost eleven, Sylvia and I persuaded our parents that we simply had to go horse riding. I cannot remember if it was agreed to as an inducement to work hard at school and pass our eleven-plus exam or as a reward for doing so. That did not matter, we could learn to ride.

Sylv went to stables near Bentley and I went to Seechem Farm, Rowney Green to be taught by Miss Quinney. Auntie Chris came up trumps and paid for my new jodhpurs, made to measure at Brough's, and Auntie Daye bought my brown, velvet-covered hard hat. For my birthday I received yellow string gloves and a leather crop with a horn handle and Granny knitted me a warm jumper as we could not afford a hacking jacket.

Each Saturday morning Dad would drive me to the farm then he and Mum would motor round the lanes while I had my one-hour lesson. By the time I left junior school I could ride to a trot and canter and we would go across the farm fields on a hack. It was wonderful and the culmination of all my dreams.

However, this was only once a week. The rest of our time at weekends and during holidays we had the most exciting times. Both our Mums worked and we were trusted to play quite a distance from home. We had the freedom to explore the wilderness behind Oldcrest, to make camps in the overgrown allotments, and to swing over the brook that separated the Gardens of Remembrance from the old cemetery. We would play ball against the side of the house, climb the walls of Sylvia's house's entry with a leg each side, we would gather treasures and store them in our secret dens and have wonderful fun. We would read our comics, the Beano, the Dandy and the Topper then swap them. Sometimes we would play doctors and nurses or opera singers. Slowly we started to grow up.

In the school holidays we would sometimes visit Sylvia's Mum at work. She was a book-binder and worked at the Redditch Indicator Works in Easemore Road. We would approach down a passage beside the Indicator stationery shop on Church Green East. We crossed several yards and passed a couple of huge buildings where we could hear the rumble of printing machines. As we approached the binding room we could hear the radio blaring away, coming over the Tannoy loudspeakers and the women would sing along with the popular songs of the day. Some of the women would look up from their stitching machines or gluing or clamping presses and point to where Sylv's Mum was working and we made our way carefully across the huge workshop. The smell was a mixture of gum, fresh paper and machine oil, all overlaid with the mineral smell of printing ink. Mrs. B would briefly stop work to check that everything was alright with Sylvia and me and sometimes she would reach beside her machine for her handbag and give us sixpence each from her purse. Sylvia's Dad was dead and I knew money was tight and so I especially appreciated always being treated equally with Sylv.

Sylvia's house was as familiar as my own and we spent our free time evenly divided between them. Number 127 had four floors. For many years there were lodgers in the attic but when they moved out it meant Sylv and her sister Mary could have separate rooms. On the ground floor there was the back kitchen with a shallow brown crock sink, a gas cooker, a kitchen cabinet and a huge work surface covered with lino. This was, in fact, the top of the bath and hinged up and hooked onto the wall when the bath was in use. The water was heated in a geyser and it was great fun to have a bath at Sylvia's house. We shared the huge bath and sat one each end, lying in the deep water and talking until the water was almost cold.

The toilet was outside, up the yard. While one of us was using the facilities, the other one would stand sociably in the corner chatting. Where the distemper had peeled off the wall in patches it formed interesting shapes and we spent many happy minutes likening these shapes to countries of the world or animals, and testing each others powers of imagination.

'Find Italy,' Sylv would instruct.

'Got it!' I would shriek while I softened the harsh toilet paper by rubbing it vigorously between my hands. 'Now you find an elephant on the ceiling.'

The living room was very cosy and there was usually a fire burning in the grate giving a comforting glow to the old armchairs, the table and chairs and the sideboard. It was taken for granted that we would always lay the table, reaching down the china from the cupboards in the alcove, and pulling open the deep heavy drawer for the cutlery. Anything perishable was kept in the cool of the cellar. As we opened the cellar door between the living room and front parlour a draught of cold air would blow out. We clicked on the light and descended the stone steps. On a shelf on the left would be cheese, butter and some vegetables. Right down the bottom where the only light was through the grating of the coal-hole we could dimly pick out raised brick plinths with tiled tops and boxes covered in coal dust.

The front parlour was kept for company or special occasions. It had a Rexene covered three piece lounge suite, a china cabinet and an upright piano. Sometimes we would have a go; hammering out Chopsticks or trying to sight-read the music from the Methodist hymnbook.

Part of the growing up process for me was spending time with Dad. His workshop was a wonderful place. I think he must have had a tool to do every single job, from soldering irons that he would bring in and heat in the flames of the gas stove, to tin snips, saws of every size and type, plastering trowels and of course electrical tools and equipment.

The things I found most interesting were his radio and telephone equipment. He had retained items from his previous employment as both a GPO telephone engineer and as a radio repairer and electrician. Piled high on the bench, the opposite end to the huge vice, were bells and cables, batteries, coils and bulbs, old telephones and circuit boards and spilling from shelves were knobs and switches and huge skeins of wire.

Every moment that I had free I wanted to be out there with Dad. Starting from when I was about nine and continuing for many years he would fit up all sorts of devices for my pleasure and education. We would have Morse code tappers, internal telephone systems, and games to move a metal loop along a kinked wire without ringing a bell. When I was a little older Dad helped me make a crystal set radio in an old cigar box. Under his supervision I hand-wound the copper coil and marked out a rudimentary dial on a piece of plywood, with studs and an old clock hand to serve as a tuning device. When the crystal and cat's whisker were in place and the heavy bakelite headphones connected by way of a brown cloth-covered, twisted flex, the excitement of hearing voices and music was indescribable.

One day Dad said we would make a periscope. He drew the design on the back of an old envelope and produced some stiff card and a reel of brown sticky-tape. Together we marked out and cut the card to size and I held it while the moistened tape dried, holding the sections together and we then had a square sectioned tube with an opening in each end on opposite sides. Dad had found a couple of handbag-sized mirrors and we slotted them in the openings and secured them at forty-five degrees so that the image would reflect down the tube from one mirror to another. I was very excited at the possibility of spying on people using this gadget but everyone soon became used to the solid brown tube protruding round corners and over walls. Another time Dad made me a kaleidoscope and I loved seeing the scattering of beads and slivers of coloured foil sweet-wrappers form intricate geometric patterns when I looked through the spy-hole.

Dad would also mend clocks and there was often an old shoe box containing all the bits and pieces from his latest project. When we finally went in to the kitchen to eat our supper, sometimes Dad would take out his mouth organ and play a few tunes.

Over the years I had my favourites and spent many happy hours sitting on Dad's lap while he leant back in the ancient rocking chair and blew into that wonderful instrument that he kept in the breast pocket of his tweed jacket.

I would learn "Under the lilacs he smoked his cigar" and "Sandy he belongs to the mill" and "Silver threads amongst the gold".

I loved and admired Dad and he loved me. We formed a very special bond. I shadowed him all the time he was at home. I never wanted to dry the dishes, put my clean clothes away or learn to dust the banisters. I wanted to be with Dad and do interesting things.

I felt comfortable when I was with Dad. He was solidly built and his clothes smelt nice. His shirt was always fresh and his baggy corduroy trousers hitched up with a leather belt and his old tweed jacket smelt reassuringly of sawdust and a slightly mineral tang of machine oil. His hair had been grey for years and he tried to tame the waviness with brilliantine. He would stand at the kitchen sink cheeks lathered up with fragrant shaving soap and brandish his cut-throat razor up and down the strop hanging on the back of the door. He perfected a close shave that was much admired by Mum and liberally splashed cologne on his cheeks.

'Have I got a clean cravat Mary?' he would query. 'The yellow and red paisley pattern would be nice.'

Mum dutifully pattered upstairs to check and produced the requested cravat knowing that Dad thought it was uncouth to be without a covering at his neck but loathed ties.

Although he carried out his ablutions in public I never saw him without his shirt. He would carefully tuck his collar inside his shirt and drape a towel round neck ready to pat up trickles of water. More personal bathing went on behind the firmly locked door of the bathroom, as it did for all our family members.

So, month by month we moved closer to the hurdle of the eleven plus examination. Happily both Sylvia and I passed, to the delight of our teacher Miss K. Harris and the pride of our headmaster Mr. Anstis – even then school statistics were important.

With excitement tinged with sadness we sang "Lord dismiss us with thy blessing" at our last assembly at St. Luke's school and prepared ourselves for the adventure of Redditch County High.

Chapter 5

∽ Collecting, making and joining ∽

The summer holidays of 1955 passed in a frenzy of uniform buying and name-tape sewing. The outfit for Redditch County High School consisted of navy-blue blazer and gymslip and white blouse, and the tie was red and blue striped. Our school hat for girls was a bizarre affair, a bit like a tam-o-shanter; a beret sort of thing, but with a band round the opening that gave a snug fit on the head. A small version of the school badge was sewn on it and showed the motto of Nihil quam optime, (which was later changed to Nil nisi optime, as someone discovered an error in the Latin translation). The motto meant "Nothing but the best", and all through our school life we were reminded that we were the top 20% of children.

Mum insisted that I had to have a hateful gabardine raincoat, double breasted, with a slit up the back which closed with a button in very bad weather. Around the wrists another button could be tightened to make the sleeves wind-tight. No one else in my class had one; it was an optional extra, and must have cost a bomb, especially as it had a button-in quilted lining. I felt very conspicuous in it and wore it as infrequently as possible.

Filled with apprehension Sylvia and I made our way on the first day and approached through the gates at the end of Grove Street. During a special assembly for new-comers we were allocated our classes. Each class was assigned an initial letter which spelt out Redditch County High School. Sylvia and I were both in 1S and our teacher was Miss Parker. It was a girls-only class with 33 of us. Looking back at that class photo today, I can put names to only fifteen girls, but besides Sylvia another was to remain a friend for life, Judith Ann Davies.

We learnt the school rules and after a few weeks had settled into the routine of work and play. Very quickly I established that I enjoyed English, Art, Geography and Biology. I was hopeless at History and French but in

Form 1S Redditch County High School 1955.
Me, front row third from the left. Miss Parker at the back.

Maths, Chemistry and Physics I struggled by, but it was very hard work. As ever, I hated P.E. and games. I had not lost my puppy fat and felt embarrassed exposing myself in my shorts. I only remember taking about six showers in five years of school life.

Homework was accepted as normal and we usually had two subjects a day. Everyone had text books for each subject and colour coded exercise books. We would struggle home with our leather satchels bulging and the strap cutting into our shoulder. Unlike many pupils today we all had individual desks in our form room and could arrange our books, pens, ink bottles and pencils as we wished.

Around this time I started accumulating collections of various things that interested me. Coins were one of my first collections and my interest had first been stimulated by Auntie Chris who holidayed abroad most years, and brought back her loose change for me. In addition to this my brother Jim travelled the world in the Royal Navy and when home on leave he brought all the coins he had collected on his voyages. My collection was never tremendously extensive but many school friends envied it.

My stamp collection began from the same sources but in addition, both aunties worked in offices that handled international post and they saved the stamps for me. Anyone else who received mail from foreign climes kept the stamps too. I loved sticking them in my album using the transparent gummed hinges and it was a matter of enormous pride to enter them in monetary value order and always perfectly straight.

I joined a stamp club and bought sets of stamps from a mail order catalogue sending postal orders that I had bought with my pocket money. My albums were my pride and joy but one day they were stolen from my desk and although I knew the culprit I could not prove it, and they never owned up.

Another item that was irresistible was the beautiful picture card inside a quarter pound packet of PG Tips tea. My collection had started rather slowly a year or so earlier with Granny Winnett saving them up for me to bring home on Saturday. Eventually I persuaded Mum to buy that brand of tea and I was very disappointed if I could not complete a set of fifty to glue in the wonderful albums. These albums, like the cards, were very attractive and the text most informative. The subjects included flowers, birds and astronomy, the latter was my favourite and is still in my possession.

When I was almost twelve my scant pocket money was stretched even further because I started building Airfix plastic kits. This hobby became something of an obsession and I worked my way through the range of planes, Stukas and Messerschmitts, Spitfires and Lancasters and all the rest. I hung them by threads from my bedroom ceiling and Mum must have once again despaired of having a ladylike daughter. I carried on despite mild disapproval to complete most of the ships as well. The Santa Maria, the Mayflower and the Golden Hind were just a few of my fleet. I worked for hours cutting out the plastic sheets of rigging and dabbing on the modellers' glue.

My need to be mistress of my destiny, well, at least, of my hobbies, meant that my interests were stimulated far and wide. I had always been an observant child and Sylvia and I joined the I-Spy club. I have seen recently that the I-Spy books are still available at newsagents but they do not have the same format, nor the same opportunity to join a club and win awards. Back in the 1950s you could buy for 6d a small book illustrated in black and white, about almost any topic from cars, trains and the street to birds, trees and farms. Your observation was developed as you looked for the items in the book. Once you had seen them, and it was a point of honour not to cheat, you ticked them off and entered the date spied. When you had completed the book you sent it to Big Chief I-Spy in London. The Indian Chief would reward his observant braves with a certificate and a notched and coloured feather to go in your headdress. If you had spent 1/- on a special coloured book it did not make any difference, still the same feather. As my headdress and my head grew bigger in the quest for promotion I had several books on the go at once. Sylvia and I were so taken up with the Red Indian analogy we solemnly pricked our fingers and swapped our blood cementing the bond of blood sisters.

Other artistic pursuits included the popular painting-by-numbers kits, but having completed a mare and foal followed by a galleon in full sail I decided that the finished result left something to be desired and thought I would have a go at something more hands on.

Dad had been digging out a huge hole in the corner of the garden for a pond and as he emptied the buckets I noticed that a lot of it was clay. I scooped up lumps of it and over a few weeks produced a selection of small pots, some formed by pressing my thumb inside the ball of clay and some by rolling the clay out into sheets, cutting it into shapes and joining them up to form square and heart-shaped pots. Given a design in poster paints and baked gently in the oven they provided presents to give for birthdays and Christmas.

My artistic skills were tested, along with my patience, by my efforts with my John Bull Printing Outfit. I fumbled for hours trying to make up lines of text from the minute rubber letters provided in the box. Once satisfied, I would ink up my sentences with the roller which I had loaded thickly with the dense black ink on the pad in the shallow tin. Biting my tongue in half with concentration I would press the lines of text onto my paper. Sometimes I would be disappointed to see that the message accompanying a picture I had painted for a card would be mis-spelt and all my efforts were for nothing.

Life was full, life was fun. What with school and homework, my collections and hobbies, long bike rides into the countryside and family excursions it seems unlikely that I could take on anything more. However my enrolment at High School meant that I could move up from Brownies and my undistinguished position in either the elves, pixies, fairies or leprechauns six to the 4th Redditch Company of the Girl Guides. Here I was a small fish in a big pond, but never-the-less, having learnt my threefold promise and a smart salute I was enrolled by Captain Meylan as a member of the Hawthorn Patrol on November 25th 1955. How I loved my copy of the Girl Guides' Handbook and I would lie awake at night planning which proficiency badges to try for and whether to aim for a Woodcraft Emblem or Little House Emblem. Really it was no contest; with my ability to light fires, tie knots and stalk a trail I thought I could live in the woods for weeks.

Looking now at my bright red tie (which could double as a sling) on which I have sewn my meagre tributes I realise I may have been spreading myself a bit thin, as I only obtained three badges. My collector's badge was a dead cert, but my artist's badge required a little fine-tuning in the presentation of my sketch book and a variety of pictures in different media. I took my horse woman's badge most seriously. I think it was equivalent to the Pony Club Grade II award and involved not only being able to ride but a knowledge of horse and stable management.

The badges were duly presented while the company ranged itself in a horseshoe around the Colours, and there I stuck without much progress for the next three or four years that I was a Guide. I became a second class guide in 1957 and a patrol second in 1958 but really I was not cut out for such a disciplined regime of routine and regulations.

I wanted to be free, roaming under the skies, riding a horse across heath land, cooking on a stick fire, wild and unfettered.

I loved family picnics, and if it was a fine day I desperately hoped we would drive out on Sunday afternoon. The answer to my plea was usually,

'Yes, get the box ready.'

The box contained all we would need to make a cup of tea: newspaper and kindling, a bottle of water and a twist of tea leaves in a scrap of greaseproof paper, four plastic mugs and a screw jar of milk. Mum came into her own when sandwiches were needed. She soon made the favourite selection of cheese and chutney, marmite and lettuce and blackcurrant jam. A few of Granny's fairy cakes shoved into a paper bag would be dessert.

We settled into the car with the box stowed in the boot with the plaid rug.

'Where will it be then?' queried Dad.

'Oh, the water splash please,' I got in quickly before my brother requested the field behind the ruined cottage near Morton Bagot.

Soon out of town, fifteen minutes driving along lanes brought us to a clearing, a sort of pull in where you collected yourself, your belongings and your animals before descending the cobbled slope to the water.

We had been coming here for years but even for a precocious teenager the magic had never evaporated. The sticklebacks still swam under the slab footbridge and we leant on the iron railing watching them dart into the reeds.

'Look for the twigs,' Dad called, and we gathered dried grass, thistle heads and sticks which we arranged in size order awaiting the striking of the first match.

'Now the forked branch for the kettle.'

I lay on the grass in my jeans and jumper, stylish frock and petticoats forgotten. Dad warned us to keep back a bit and suddenly the sports page of the Sunday paper flared up and caught the dried grass and seed heads. We patiently fed the fire, the pile of waiting sticks diminishing as the flames grew taller and hotter. Dad rammed the forked stick into the soil and let the bottom of the sooty kettle touch the now glowing twigs.

The blanket was spread out, packets of sandwiches opened up and Mum sat back leaving Dad to organise her cuppa. The kettle began to sing and the tea leaves were tipped in and left to brew. We were soon sipping it from the orange cups and flicking midges away from our sandwiches. After having a paddle and walking along the hedge where the May blossom cast its sickly scent it was time to pack everything away.

As we emptied the tealeaves onto the dying fire we knew another treat was in store. We drove slowly across the ford and Steve and I begged Dad to stop in the middle of the river, but Mum urged,

'Quick Jim, in case we conk out.'

My mother's love of nature and wide knowledge of country lore helped to make these days special and reinforced my feelings. I sometimes felt that she too longed to be free and that her wild and romantic imagination had been dominated by family responsibilities.

My father's influence was enormous too. We would stand in the yard behind our house looking up to the night sky watching for meteors and comets and I would learn the names of the constellations glimpsed through the binoculars. Dad would talk of the possibility of life on other planets and of how they were formed. He would tell me his theories about the evolution of mankind, the formation of personality, philosophy and abstract thought. He encouraged me to read his favourite authors, Jules Verne, H.G. Wells and Aldous Huxley. A heady mixture for an adolescent girl in the 1950s and inevitably these times were punctuated by more prosaic moments such as homework and school life and an unwilling involvement in housework.

I was still very much involved in the church and now I was allowed to attend social functions accompanied by Sylvia, her sister and mother.

We had a Saturday night social most months and competed in quizzes, beetle drives and treasure hunts. Sometimes there was an opportunity to dance or perform, according to your particular talent. Sylv and I had received glove puppets one Christmas and like most children enjoyed taking on a different persona. We quickly learnt that a puppet could voice feelings that we ourselves may not be able to articulate. We made more puppets out of papier-mâché and painted lurid features and fixed their hand-stitched clothes with a rubber band to a groove we had formed round their neck. Our puppet shows were in great demand. We would crouch behind a big table, turned on its side, a table cloth draped over, and bring to life the Cisco Kid and Pancho and Mexican Pete. We would mould witches and fairies and make up plays that involved singing or fighting or both.

Sylvia and I also joined the church choir and sat in the special pews each side of the communion table. We learnt The Messiah, The Creation and other sacred songs. The choir had pride of place during the many anniversaries of the church year.

Saturdays were taken up with horses. Both Sylv and I now rode at Mrs. Elwell's stables in Green Lane, Studley. How we envied her two daughters Ann and Susan. They had permanent access to a field of ponies. We would book our lesson for mid-morning and fly hell-for-leather on our bikes down the Slough from Crabbs Cross.

We wanted to arrive in time to catch our mounts, stable and groom them, lift the spotless and supple bridles from the pegs and gently put the bit over the horse's tongue. We would lift the saddles from the strong saddle racks and carefully place them on the horse's back and tighten the girth. Other pupils would arrive but they were happy to be less involved. We would take our horses through their paces in the fenced-off riding school in the field, and then maybe ride round the lanes or through Terry's woods.

After our hour, when the horses were stripped of tack, we might rub them down and turn them out in the paddock. Then we could muck out the loose boxes and wheel steaming barrows to the muck heap.

We dreamt horses, drew horses and read horsy books. We gave each other Beswick china models of foals for birthdays and our wooden shadow-box display shelves were filled with every type of horse, wooden, china or plastic. We pleaded for new items of equestrian attire for Christmas and birthdays and longed to become Pony Club members.

One day, as we became friendlier with the Elwell family we were invited to participate in a gymkhana. There was a trotting race for me and an obstacle race for Sylvia. Although I did not win a coveted rosette I thought I would burst with excitement.

In the summer of 1957, just a short while after my thirteenth birthday, something remarkable happened. My parents decided that we would go to Butlins for our annual holiday. Up until now all our holidays had been in Hastings. Each year we would visit Grandma Ancell, Auntie Stella and the rest of the family at Braybrooke Road. We would somehow all bump up together and cram into the limited space. This year was to be different. Butlins Holiday Camps were widely advertised and their logo was a familiar sight on commercial television and in newspapers and magazines. After much poring over brochures we finally decided on the camp at Filey in Yorkshire. To my great delight Mum said we could invite my very best friend, Sylvia, to join us.

After a long journey over unfamiliar roads we eventually arrived at the camp. Passing through the grand gates we joined the queue to be allocated our chalets. Mum, Dad and Steve would share one and Sylv and I would be next door. We loved it. There were fairground rides, roller skating, swimming, puppet shows and all the rest of the fun to be experienced and best of all we could go round the site on our own. We went horse riding every day and once Dad took us fossil hunting on a nearby beach.

However, it was an experiment never to be repeated. My parents hated it. They hated the noisy clash of cutlery and the hub-bub of excited voices in the communal dining hall. They hated their chalet, unfortunately positioned between the toilet block and the nursery. Most of all they hated being told when to wake up, when to go for meals and the incessant voice over the Tannoy which highlighted events taking place throughout the camp. To cap it all, it rained every day. Sylvia and I hardly noticed it in our eager attempts to try everything that the camp offered.

Mum and Dad had witnessed enough and decided that we would leave a day early. Feeling very disappointed we packed our bags and hauled them to the car-park. Driving home my parents dissected the whole ghastliness of the holiday that they had thought would be so wonderful. The worst of it was, Mum said, was that it was 'common'. There was nothing else to say after that. From then on Hastings was the normal destination for the Claysmith family each summer.

Life continued with its highs and lows and was punctuated by important family events.

Granny and Grandad Winnett celebrated their Golden wedding anniversary in 1957 and we had a special tea and their house was filled with bouquets of congratulatory flowers.

My eldest brother Jim was engaged to be married. His fiancée Ann Rix lived in Gosport near to where he was stationed. She was a very pretty young woman and as slim as a lath. They had a long engagement and did not get married until 1960.

Rosemary married Maurice Reeves in June of 1957. He came from the village of Studley and Mum was pleased he was a white-collar worker, employed as a clerk in the Redditch Building Society.

My other sister, Jean, had become disenchanted with both nursing and teaching and decided she had a vocation to become a nun. She entered the Anglican Convent of the Holy Name at a village near Malvern, and began her training as a novice in quite a strict order.

Outwardly, as far as I knew we were a normal working class family with aspirations. My parents both worked hard, ploughed their money into their home, garden and family and were very much the leading lights of the social scene within their group of friends

They would host parties and play cards. I would creep out of bed in my pyjamas and sit at the top of the stairs, head almost through the banisters, trying to catch the conversation. There was laughter and music, the chink of glasses. Everyone was there; Auntie Chris and Uncle Bert, Fred and Christine, Auntie Freda and Ada, Smudger and Agnes and sometimes Dad's Irish mate from work was roped in to add an extra strand of fun. Sometimes if they heard me I might be allowed downstairs to sit next to Dad or sip someone's drink.

Everything was going well for us Claysmiths. I had reached fourteen and still had no inkling that lurking behind this front of conformity and social acceptance was a well kept secret, but I did not begin to suspect this for another four years.

Chapter 6

∞ Boys and God, horses and dancing ∞

In my fourth year at Redditch County High I realised that I had better start taking school seriously. Before the summer holiday I had made decisions about what subjects to study, ready for the General Certificate of Education 'O' level examinations. I had dropped Physics, French and History but we were encouraged to take a wide range of subjects to give us a broad academic base.

My ambition for many years had been to become a veterinary surgeon. Unfortunately, I realised too late that because I had not been in a class that studied Latin, an essential subject for doctors and vets alike, I would never catch up before 'O' levels. I had to think again about my career.

I was torn two ways, and tried to keep my options open. I had quite a talent for art in all its forms, and thought I might become a commercial artist, illustrator or interior designer. On the other hand, what of my love of animals and of my good marks in biology? I decided to take both arts and science subjects and delay the decision for as long as possible.

There was lots of homework and inevitably some of my adolescent interests faded away. However they were soon replaced by others. I hurried through my homework before six o'clock tea so that I could go out.

I baby-sat regularly for Auntie Freda's daughter, Janet, and her husband Robert while they went ballroom dancing. I felt responsible and confident looking after baby Belinda. After I had been doing this job for about a year I took advantage of the freedom and used to invite boyfriends round for company and supper.

One evening a week was the prayer meeting at church, and one was choir practice.

It was Friday nights that I really looked forward to: Youth Club. We had a choice of activities, billiards or snooker on a full sized table, table tennis or

Me 1960, Fifth form, Redditch County High School.

darts. When not taking part in a game we would play records on the portable Dansette or fool around with the boys.

Boys did not have much impact on me until I was turned fifteen. Then I realised that their lives were much more fun than girls'. They had more freedom, could stay out later and were trusted more. They had opinions and the confidence to voice them, even if it was of load of guff.

The boys in my class at school could not be taken seriously on the whole. Familiarity seemed to breed contempt. They were just kids I had grown up with, but there were a few I fancied from afar. They were usually sixth-formers and unattainable as boy friends. They usually played in the school band or the cricket first-eleven or maybe were handsome boys from other classes in the same year as me. Sometimes Headless Cross boys from youth club were the focus of attention and like many teenage girls my fantasies were fuelled by comics of the time, with photo-strips featuring romantic stories.

Apart from harmless games like postman's knock and sardines, the nearest I got to a boy was running round the block with the rest of the gang, or daringly cycling back and forth outside a boy's house, hoping he would notice me. The annual Cherry Wake fair and the Redditch Carnival funfair were two possibilities for more serious contact in the form of a snog or embrace behind the coconut shy or cuddling up close on the ghost train.

I did develop a crush on one darkly handsome boy and sent him anonymous valentine and birthday cards. There was not a flicker of interest and my ardour was never reciprocated.

Everything seemed so innocent then, and in any case we were all told that a kiss could lead to an embrace, and it was not a big jump to full-on sex, and we all knew what happened to girls like that. And it quite often did! Contraception was not available and it was only the very daring who got down to it in the back of a car. Needless to say my parents were constantly worried about what I had been up to but in fact my morals were self-regulating in line with the teaching of the church, but it did not stop the urge.

I suffered the usual teenage insecurities, along with most of my friends. I was not happy with the way I looked but I reckoned that I had two redeeming features. One of these was my hair which had changed from the mousey grey-brown that developed after I had lost my little-girl blondness. It was now a quite nice dark brown, and curly. Trouble was I wanted straight hair. I felt I could have a greater range of styles if my hair had been straight. Anyway, not only that but it had a fine texture and got greasy very quickly. Mum said I should only wash it twice a week or it would get worse. Once I had found that a beer shampoo in little brown, plastic barrels suited it and gave up wanting straight hair I decided my hair was quite nice!

The other feature that was passable was my eyes. Like all of my family, on both sides, I had blue eyes and mine were quite pale but intense, not a watery blue. As I grew up I realised that I may as well accept what I had and not waste too much energy or anxiety on something I could never have.

Earlier I said boys usually had the confidence to voice their opinions but about this time my debating skills had chance to develop.

After church on Sunday evenings young people aged fifteen to twenty one were invited round to the minister's house for the Epworth Fellowship, named after the village where John Wesley was born. Crammed into the study, balancing hot drinks on our knees we would discuss the rights and wrongs of all sorts of subject; sex before marriage, contraception and abortion, capital punishment, the holy trinity, life after death and the atom bomb. One Easter the senior youth club performed a play about Hiroshima and Nagasaki.

I became a Sunday school teacher taking responsibility for a primary class and attending the teacher's seminars one evening a week. The lessons across the whole age range were linked by a common topic and very carefully controlled by the use of the Teacher's Guide text book. I also belonged to the International Bible Reading Association and with the help of a themed booklet I read the bible every day. In 1958 I had become a junior member of the Methodist church, a very solemn moment.

To counterbalance this there were fun moments of course. Once a year, usually on May Bank Holiday, there was a church outing not to be missed: a day out in Malvern.

We would catch the train to Great Malvern, changing at Worcester, carrying bags of sandwiches and wearing strong shoes. We would walk up through the town and ascend the lane which led to St. Anne's Well on the side of the Worcestershire Beacon. At this point we all needed to take a breather so we would have a drink of spring water using the cup on a chain. The well house was and still is, a sturdy and quaint building nestling in a sheltered hollow.

After this short rest we would continue our ascent of the Beacon huffing and puffing all the way up its 1,394 feet. On the summit was the wonderful Beacon Café, a wooden shack with a steaming tea urn and small packets of biscuits in cellophane and slices of cake under plastic domes. Around the walls were framed photographs of the hills. We were all glad to move out of the wind and bundled in to sit on the benches.

Then we began the walk along the crest of the ridge. We stretched out in a gaggle, about twenty of us. By then we would be splitting up into groups. Sylv and I inseparable as usual, would walk together and maybe be joined by Dave Woods and Pecker Hemming. Sylvia's sister Mary would be with her two friends Heather Brazil and Val Parsons. The older ones stuck together, Les Richards, Donald Parsons and Sylvia Macey, who all went on to theological college, were often in a group. The others would pick up the threads in any conversation.

Down into the Wyche cutting, a brief visit to the toilets, then on. Up and down, up and down the switch-back. The view was tremendous; Worcester and Pershore with its Abbey, across the Vale of Evesham, beyond Bredon Hill and up the Cotswold escarpment. On a particularly good day you might see Broadway Tower. To the west were the lush fields of Herefordshire and uncharted territory. Sometimes we would see the smoke from a train as it disappeared into the Colwall tunnel.

Later in the day we would cross the Ross on Wye to Upton upon Severn road, maybe stopping at the roadside snack cabin for a chocolate bar. The walk was nearing completion. Just the earthworks of the British Camp now, crowning the Herefordshire Beacon. We looked down from the ramparts to the lake below and imagined life in the Bronze Age.

Once at the top of this easier climb we could relax a while and have a proper rest. All our sandwiches were eaten and bottles of pop were guzzled. There was nothing left but to turn tail from the windy plateau that formed the summit and begin the return journey.

We walked back along the road in the lee of the hills, on a lower contour. We would sing songs to keep us going and step out at a swinging pace to cover up our tiredness.

Back in town, if there was time to spare before our train home, we would visit the marble halls of the Pump Room at the Winter Gardens. We sipped spa-water from the huge metal cups and absorbed the Edwardian atmosphere of the fern-filled room. Through the French windows was a terrace and steps leading to the beautiful Winter Gardens. There were shrubs and flowers of interest even in the dullest months. A bridge crossed the boating lake and little paths led into secret corners. It was a magical end to a wonderful day.

Finally we trudged slowly back to the railway station with its beautiful canopy and decorated cast iron pillars to take a gentle ride home in a steam train.

My friends from church formed a very important part of my life. We all followed each other's progress with interest. Two of the older members, Donald and Les had gone to college to train to become ministers. One of their contemporaries back home was Graham. We all fancied him, us teenage girls. He was a bit old for us but that did not matter. It was only a dream, a fantasy.

There was not much to base our fantasies on at that time. Only the pimply sixth-formers in the cricket first-eleven or an older brother-in-law or the people we met at youth club. But Graham, well, he was older and he smiled, my how he smiled. He was not a thin rake and his relaxed, handsome face would crease up and the corners of his mouth would crinkle.

He was the organist at church and all the girls in the choir fancied him. His father was the local piano-tuner and that was from whom Graham had learnt his knowledge and love of music. There were nights when he would relax, drop the responsibility of the choir and organ, and become an essential part of the fun. On the fourth Saturday of the month were the church socials and Graham was in great demand to play the piano. He would tinkle away in the background while the chat went on and then he would strike up for the dances. He could do anything: the Valetta, the Military

Quickstep, the Waltz or the Gay Gordons. He would accompany anyone who wanted to sing to us and he had played the music when years ago, Sylvia and I had done our puppet shows.

He was warm, cosy, comfortable and unattainable. Then one year, Heather told me they were engaged. She was nineteen and at teacher's training college. We guessed, Sylv and me, that Graham was at least ten years older. But that did not matter. Heather had got him and he was not free anymore. Luckily by this time our fantasies had moved on and we both had our own boyfriends.

When I was in the fifth year at school I investigated the possibility of jobs for women in practical farming. I had never fancied a conventional job and the idea of becoming a herdswoman on a dairy farm held great appeal. I imagined myself living in a caravan in the corner of a field. This was typical accommodation, close to the herd and accessible for emergencies and early morning milking. If not that, another job with farming connections, maybe a milk recorder working for the Ministry. I contacted the three agricultural colleges that accepted women and in due course they sent their prospectus.

Studley College, a mere four miles away, was a women-only college and I discounted it immediately. In any case I would be expected to continue living at home and I did not want that. By the time I was ready for college I would want to make my own decisions and get away from the claustrophobic atmosphere of home.

The University College of Wales at Aberystwyth offered a course, but surprisingly their educational requirements were not as demanding as colleges that specialised in agriculture.

I liked the sound of Seale-Hayne college in Devon. The standards were high; it had a good reputation and was single minded in its approach to agriculture. For entrance to the course, The Diploma in Dairying, you had to gain six 'O' level passes and work in practical farming for at least eighteen months. I could delay my final decision again and also keep my options open. I completed an application and arranged an interview.

Farming attracted me and a close friend from youth club, named Jane Adams, and I decided to join the local Young Farmers Club at Alvechurch. They met on Wednesday evenings and were a lively gang. We went there on the bus but usually got driven home.

We would have talks on all aspects of farming and country life, take part in quizzes, go on farm walks and learn to judge stock. Best of all were the socials or hops in the village hall where we would dance to the latest records or if our club was hosting a proper dance, when club members from all over the county were invited, we would have a small band to play. I was a member until I was eighteen, and left home, but it was not until I had left school that I was allowed to go to dances at locations throughout Worcestershire, partnered by a boy.

I could not dance, at least only the Valetta and Military Two-step, so I thought I had better learn, ready. Just before I was sixteen I ventured down our road to a beginners' class in ballroom dancing, conveniently at a dance studio about one hundred yards away.

I felt nervous and conspicuous but at the end of the ten week course I had learnt to waltz, quickstep and cha-cha. Full of enthusiasm I signed on for the improvers' class. The foxtrot and jive followed, plus more impressive footwork for the earlier dances. I was hooked and loved it.

My cotton skirt was puffed out with three petticoats, a soft one to prevent my stockings becoming snagged, a multi-layered net one with satin trimmings and a starched broiderie anglais one on top. Swishing around that dance floor I felt the bee's knees. By the time I was allowed to go to proper dances I could join in without shame. My parents must have entertained the hope that at least I was now becoming a young lady.

I had been quite strictly brought up but I did not always conform to the code of behaviour expected of me.

'Put your legs down, Angie,'

'Sit with your knees together,'

'Angela, pull your skirt down.'

The list of transgressions was enormous. I could not be myself and often felt my personality was being taken over. Dad seemed more content with the way I was growing up but Mum always wanted more or better.

I often got a clip round my ear for misbehaving or a sharp dab on the leg if I did not cover my knees up and for serious crimes Mum would defer to Dad.

'Wait until I tell your father what you've done. He'll give you a good walloping,' she warned.

She would relate the tale to Dad when he returned home from work and he would have to work himself up enough to give me a stern ticking off.

Sometimes he did not need Mum's prompting and laid into me with a slipper, one whack for every stair I ran up. It must have been serious for him to do that because Dad believed in shaming me with words and making me realise that I had done wrong. The guilt would do the rest.

Mum was strict about other things too. She said headaches and stomach aches did not exist.

'You'll soon forget about it when you get to school,' she would argue. To prove the point, at teatime she would say,

'How's your headache?

'What headache?' I usually replied.

Another favourite saying was,

'If you are well enough to stand up, you are well enough to go to school.'

Music of all sorts had begun to have an impact on me. From the mid 1950s at home we had a record-player with a Garrard deck and fancy auto-change. At that stage I did not have any records of my own but used to listen to Rosemary's. There was Mario Lanza singing songs from the Student Prince, Frankie Laine, Connie Francis, the Boswell Sisters, Dean Martin and Frank Sinatra. She even had, or should I say, inevitably had, some Elvis numbers on 78's. 'Heartbreak Hotel' and 'One night with you' were the first I heard. I was entranced. As soon as I could save some money I bought more records, especially by Elvis. If I could not buy them I listened on the radio. Radio Luxembourg on 207m was the best station.

My close friend Judy Davies and her friend Viv were very informed about the latest tracks. At home Sylvia and I would play records over and over to learn the words and sing along with Guy Mitchell, Tommy Steele and Lonnie Donegan. We would swoon at the sheer sexiness of Elvis Presley and Roy Orbison. Buddy Holly had a wonderful plaintive voice and we soon had the words off pat.

Songs from the musicals were also learnt by heart. We watched Oklahoma, West Side Story, Seven Brides for Seven Brothers and Calamity Jane.

Biblical epics were a 'must see' category of film too, for their moral content and special effects. 'The Robe' and 'The Ten Commandments' had quite an impact on our impressionable minds and we soaked up graphic details of miracles. In fact cinema going was a big thing for me.

There were four cinemas to choose from in Redditch; the Danilo, the Gaumont, the Regal and the Palace. The programme usually changed three times a week and whenever possible we tried to go twice but rarely missed at least one visit weekly. Our heroes were Cary Grant and Rock Hudson, Dirk

Bogarde and Burt Lancaster. We loved to emulate the tomboy Doris Day and admired the sophisticated James Mason. What a wonderful escape it was from Redditch, school and home.

Escape was to be had in more ordinary ways too. I was trusted to go into Birmingham by train or on the 147 bus and I would do the rounds, C&A, Lewis's, Rackham's and Dorothy Perkins. The day came when I was allowed to choose a new coat. This was the first item of clothing that had not been selected by Mum. Sylvia already had her first grown-up coat in emerald green wool, closely fitting at the waist and with wide sleeves that narrowed to a buttoned cuff. Now it was my turn and it took me all day to find one I liked. Finally I selected a loose-fitting swagger coat in a beautiful pinky red colour. It hung down from my shoulders in a gentle swirl and I took it home for approval. It passed the test: a twirl in front of Mum to make sure it wasn't 'common' and I could wear it to church on Sunday with my cream shoes and gloves.

From this time on I was trusted to buy other new clothes and also my underwear. Both my friend and I wore elasticated roll-on girdles with suspenders on the bottom for our stockings and purchased at Dorothy Perkins for 4/11d. (25p).

Young people at this time did not have much opportunity to exercise their personal choice either in clothes, food or their bedrooms. We were expected only to go into our bedroom to change our clothes or go to bed. In any case there was no heating so it was rather a bleak place to be. Teenagers in the late 1950s had just started to have the teeniest breakthrough in matters of style and I longed to have a co-ordinated bedroom with wallpaper that I had chosen. Eventually I persuaded my parents to buy a very contemporary paper in yellow and black on a muddy-looking background. It owed something to the jungle and animal prints with its columns of jagged slashes of colour and Mum and Dad hated it. I was disappointed that I had to keep the same bedroom suite which had been handed down by Auntie Daye. It was an angular 1930 style suite in limed oak and had ziggurat shapes in green wood on the corners. Still, one step at a time. I had managed to exchange my pink paisley-patterned eiderdown for a slightly more stylish candlewick bedspread in yellow.

Sometimes I would visit Granny Winnett at Alcester and stay for a few days. Auntie Chris would take me on shopping expeditions to Stratford upon Avon and occasionally to Worcester.

Auntie Daye had remarried in the 1950s and her new husband was her boss from the Austin Motor Company. They owned a beautiful bungalow at Cookhill not far from where she and her sisters had been brought up. In the holidays I used to go on the bus and spend a pleasant day in the country with Auntie and the two Dachshunds, Karl and Petre.

Every year my parents, Steve and I would visit Grandma Ancell and the rest of the family in Hastings. The highlights of the visit would be the firework displays in Alexandra Park on Wednesday evenings and a journey up the cliff railway to the West Hill to visit the castle famous for its 1066 connections. We would also walk along Bottle Alley underneath the Promenade. The walls were entirely covered with shards of coloured glass from thousands of bottles, and embedded in cement. They were arranged in patterns and with the sun shining on them they would glint and sparkle in a glorious way.

Once when returning to Redditch from Hastings by our usual route we made a detour from High Wycombe to West Wycombe. From quite a distance Dad pointed out a church perched on a hill. On top of the church tower, gleaming in the sun was a golden ball. Not being able to judge the scale I assumed it was part of a fancy weather vane. As we drove closer Dad said,

'We're going to visit that church Angie, and we might be able to go up the tower.'

Mum quickly decided she would wait below with Steve. Once the car was parked Dad escorted me with his slow amble towards the church. The building was empty but surprisingly access to the tower was unrestricted. We climbed the steps slowly and emerged into the sunlight. I was amazed! The ball which had seemed just a speck from a mile away was about ten feet across. My heart beat fast in anticipation when Dad showed me a ladder leading up to a doorway on the side of the golden ball. Carefully we climbed the steps and heaved ourselves into the wooden structure. Dad told me the history of this awesome building.

The church had been rebuilt in the eighteenth century by Sir Francis Dashwood to satisfy his eccentric interests. Against the conventional background of the landed gentry living in a Palladian style mansion he had sought other diversions and founded the Hell Fire Club. This wooden ball perched on the top of the church tower was where ten of the members would meet. Dad hinted at satanic rites, orgies and wild drinking parties. My imagination fired up as we descended the stairs to reality, and picnicked near the impressive ruined mausoleum of the Dashwood family.

Meanwhile, the dreaded 'o' level exams loomed. Despite trying very hard I was falling behind in both Chemistry and Maths. They were two of the named subjects essential for college entrance and I had to pass them. I was seriously worried. The subject teachers came to the rescue. On two lunch-breaks a week I had extra tuition, Don Yapp for chemistry and Jimmy Morrall for maths. I almost did formulae and equations in my sleep and algebra and trigonometry over my breakfast.

There was no going back. Towards the end of the fifth year, at just turned sixteen I took my General Certificate of Education, ordinary level, examinations.

There was a sense of relief when they were over. We had cricket matches and tennis tournaments and a school dance. Finally, when term had ended, I went on a week long camping holiday to Amroth in Pembrokeshire and waved my school days goodbye. I was growing up at last.

Chapter 7

❧ Farming ❧

During my last term at school there had raged the battle between art and farming as a career. My artistic abilities were slightly tinged with romantic notions despite the fact that I knew if I followed art as a career it would have to be commercial art, possibly in a design studio. My parents were against me and asked how I thought I would earn a living doing this. Their expectations of me were very high. I felt that whatever I did, I had to succeed, all their hopes were pinned on me. I had been to High School. I must not waste my ability. In reality my schooling was hard work and had been a real effort for me. However, they were not prepared to stand by and watch me fail. Art represented failure, so I had to aim for the other option.

I do not think they were very keen on farming either, at least not the basic sort that I wanted to do. Never mind, it consoled them to think that I might marry a farmer and become a member of the land-owning class, so they gave their approval for me to start my pre-college practical training.

I had scoured the 'Farmers' Weekly' magazine and knew the routine. I would have to work as a general farm worker or farm pupil whilst gaining experience. I found an advertisement in our local paper for a job at the farm of Joe Beckett at Brockhill on the outskirts of Redditch. I had been for an interview and had been accepted once my parents had paid a fee of £50 for a year's apprenticeship.

I got kitted up ready to begin work: good quality Wellington boots, strong lace-up shoes, two pairs of tough jeans and a leather, ex war-department jerkin belted tight with my Girl Guide belt. Layers of shirts and jumpers were needed for the winter and the lot was topped with my riding mac. I felt ready to go out into the world of work and make my own decisions and my own mistakes.

I used to envy boys, but now I wondered why. There was not anything they could do that I could not. I was endowed with common sense, I was strong and I was confident.

One morning in early September 1960 I cycled down Hewell Road past the Swimming Baths then up Brockhill Lane as far as I could. I then pushed my bike up the very steep section thinking this would be the pattern for the next year.

Starting time was 7.30am and I had allowed half an hour for the journey. As I dismounted and pushed my bike into the farm yard to the accompaniment of cows mooing from the milking shed I felt a combination of excitement and trepidation.

Limited introductions followed as milking time was still in progress. There was George Williams the head herdsman aided by Reg the under-cowman. I watched in fascination as the clusters of teat-cups were applied to the cow's udders and the steady chug of the vacuum pump eased the milk into a huge stainless-steel bucket connected by black rubber tubing. I followed Reg into the adjoining dairy and watched him mount a couple of metal steps and pour a bucket of milk into a wide hopper. It trickled slowly over the corrugated surface of the water filled cooler and was funnelled into a ten gallon milk churn.

After half an hour of observing, milking time was over and I helped release the chains from the cow's necks. I watched them back out from the concrete standings and slowly file down the central passage of the cowshed into the yard. I picked my way carefully out of the mucky shed into the cool, clean dairy wondering if anyone was going to explain anything or give me a job to do.

When finally George paused to speak to me I could not understand a word. I had never come across a dialect like it. Over the next few months I learnt that canna, didna and wudna were sort of negative verbs and that George was from Staffordshire. I got used to working with him and learnt mainly from observation as he was, thankfully, a man of few words, who did not suffer fools gladly, and felt that if a woman had a place in farming then it was collecting eggs or cooking breakfast.

Reg's accent was easier to understand; a rounded Yorkshire that I was familiar with.

I watched as the cow muck was shovelled into piles and forked onto a trailer, the milk churns were carted to the raised platform ready for the milk lorry and the dairy equipment dismantled and scrubbed scrupulously clean in huge galvanised troughs full of near boiling water and a liberal scoop of caustic soda.

'Go with Reg now,' George ordered. 'Get the cows out.'

Reg had the yard gate open and the cows were jostling for their positions, always the same, to file up the lane.

'Get moving. Come on, get up there.' Was Reg speaking to me or the cows?

Feeling very unsure I walked behind the huge animals stepping back swiftly if I saw their tails lift. Reg and I followed the herd and he suggested I cut a hazel twig to flick the hind quarters of cows who slowed down to graze the roadside grass. The leader turned into the open gate and finally they were all in the field. We latched the gate and walked back with Reg asking me a few questions on the way.

'Breakfast now. Come with me,' George shouted from a dark doorway in the barn. We crossed the yard to a semi-detached house and I sat with George while his wife fried us eggs to eat with thick slices of bread and butter. After the statutory thirty-minute break the dog and I were called to heel and we ambled back to the farm buildings.

'Time to mix the feed,' George grunted by way of explanation. Back through the barn door and we were in a dark, dusty room with metal hoppers poking through the plank ceiling. We tramped up rickety stairs and I watched as George heaved enormous hessian sacks across the floor to the hoppers. He tipped in flaked maize, sugar beet pulp, linseed oil cake and concentrated additives. Back downstairs a pull on a cord released a shutter and a mound of pungent smelling, dusty cattle food cascaded onto the floor.

George spat on his hands, coughed and spat on the pile.

'Canya use a shovel?'

Without waiting for an answer he started to turn the pile onto an empty space on the pitted concrete floor.

'Turn it twice, then come and find me.'

I was glad of something to do and a chance to collect my thoughts, and having adjusted my eyes to the murky interior got on with my job.

After half an hour had passed George's silhouette cast a spare shadow in the doorway.

'I've got the boss,' he stated shortly, and moving aside he indicated Mr Beckett, the owner of this and another farm.

'Good morning Angela. Are you settling in?' He asked in his rather high pitched voice. 'Come on, I'll show you round.'

His cavalry twill trousers, well polished brown brogues and Harris Tweed jacket together with a Vyella shirt and tan tie signalled him as a gentleman farmer. His piercing eyes, scouring every corner and his canny observations made me guess that he had his finger on the pulse of his farm.

'Get here alright?' he questioned, not wanting or expecting an answer. 'Right then, through here to the bull pens. In a few months you'll be leading this one round the show ring.' He nodded towards a thick set beast, already ringed through the nose.

'Out of one of our best milkers, by a great sire.'

He strode on to the next enclosure.

'Worth his weight in gold, old Ajax,' he briefly grinned with relish. 'Calf houses over there, to over-winter them until the spring grass is ready.' He gestured loosely at the range of buildings across the top of the yard, smelly rivulets oozing from beneath the doors.

Into the main barn now, which soared high to the rafters in the middle. Sweet hay was stacked in one bay, straw in the other and implements shrouded in oily tarpaulins crouching between the enormous doors.

'Met Hans yet? I expect he'll be in the weaner house.'

I trotted behind as he paced on, head bent low, tweed cap catching the fine drizzle. The smell changed as we approached the pig unit. A more acid, concentrated aroma greeted us, together with the continuous squeal of pigs.

'Farrowing pens over there, weaners here and fattening shed against the barn,' he guided my eyes across the range of low buildings with louvred ventilation hatches on their ridges.

'Hans!' he barked into a doorway. A wiry, sandy haired man wearing faded overalls appeared, his eyebrows and moustache coated in the fine dust of milled pig food.

'This is the new girl. She'll be with you for a couple of months next year.'

'Pleased to meet you Miss,' Hans ventured in his careful middle European accent.

'Do you like pigs? The cleanest animal there is.' Pride was obvious in his voice.

Prize giving day 1961 Agricultural Award Redditch College
of Further Education.

The tour was almost over, just a cursory glance at the tractor shed and diesel pumps, the Dutch barns with curved, red painted iron roofs and we were back to the cow shed.

'I'm off now George. Have those milk-yield figures ready by Thursday,' Mr Beckett called into the echoey shed.

'Yes boss,' the herdsman agreed to his employer's back as the boss walked towards his Mk II Jag. A slight contemptuous toss of George's head was evident as he beckoned me to follow and slouched back to his empire.

'Canya chop sticks, wench?' he asked doubtfully, as he indicated a pile of old boards in the corner of the boiler room.

'We heat the water for the dairy in that stove. Wood starts it, coke keeps it going. Get that done and we'll go in for our dinner.'

I was left to squat down with a sharp chopper and transform a pile of wood into neat eight inch sticks like the ones on a sheet of rusty iron next to the stove. I noticed the sticks had sawn ends so I used my initiative and reached for a saw hanging on a nail. I sawed the boards across their width to the right size then split each piece into half a dozen sticks, thanking Dad for allowing me to develop my practical skills.

My sandwiches were eaten in Mrs William's kitchen and once we had downed our mugs of tea it was obvious that George expected a doze. I excused myself and went outside to explore, feeling very conspicuous as the new girl, but at least my boots were muddy now.

Between one thirty and three o'clock I was detailed to accompany Old George, the general farm worker. He straightened his back briefly to see what he was in for, and his leer exposed gaps in his blackened teeth.

'Best get started girl. Shoulder they tools,' he nodded towards a shovel, fork and rake. He slung a bill hook, slasher and bucket into a wheelbarrow and set off across a field to the ditch we were to clear out.

He lit a Woodbine, holding it between a grimy, calloused thumb and a horny finger. He lowered himself into the overgrown ditch and looked up from under the greasy peak of his threadbare cap.

'Just for today you can watch and pass me things. You'll get dirty soon enough,' he smirked, comparing my obviously new jeans to his rickety legs encased in filthy leather gaiters down to his hobnailed boots.

After an hour or so he pulled out his pocket watch.

'Get on back now; you'll be needed for milking.'

Glad to get my circulation going I stomped across the wet field and saw the heads of the milk herd above the hedge as Reg ushered them into the collecting yard, ready to stream into the milking shed.

'They'll take some washing today,' he observed, eying the muddy udders. 'I'll show you how.'

Very soon I was confidently moving from cow to cow with a bucket of hot water and Chloros to carefully wash the mud from udders and teats. I was soon aware that this warm massaging had the effect of making the cows release their milk.

For two hours George and Reg worked as a team, feeding each cow its individual ration, applying the milking cluster and carrying the milk to the dairy.

'Your job tomorrow girl. Washing the tits and carting the milk,' George explained. 'Reg 'as got to get the pens ready for the autumn calvers. Go on, you'd better get off. We'll finish up.'

It was five fifteen, a quarter of an hour past my finishing time. I was so tired I do not know how I cycled home especially as the last mile and a half were up hill.

Mum was back from work already.

'Come on dear, strip all that mucky stuff off in the back porch. I'll see to it.' She held out my dressing gown. 'Go and have a bath, then you can tell me all about it.'

My first day as a farm apprentice was over. For the next two years a pattern of work would develop through the seasons and across the whole range of the British climate.

My ingrained work ethic became fine tuned. I learnt to enjoy work for work's sake. I loved the practical aspect of learning new skills and the pleasure of a job well done. I blossomed in the one-ness of nature, the variety and scope of the tasks and the chance to use my initiative. I thrived on having an unconventional job and avidly related anecdotes to friends and family.

My favourite place for recounting these tales was at the Sunday dinner table. Steve would sit goggle eyed as I told of calves being born, sometimes helped out by attaching ropes to their legs. Dad would dart me a warning glance.

'That'll do now dear.'

But I would continue with the story of the knacker's wagon arriving and a carcass being winched up the sloping tail-board to be carted off for pet food.

Thump! Dad's fist smashed down on the table making gravy slop from the plates.

'I said that's enough, Angela. Stop!'

But for now I was glad to soak in the bath and know that tomorrow would bring new and exciting experiences.

During the summer holidays my GCE results had arrived. I had passed in five subjects but failed the two most important ones, the two I had always struggled with, Maths and Chemistry. I had to pass them but the only college where I could study at evening class and re-sit these exams was at Bromsgrove, six miles away.

On two evenings a week I had to leave the farm promptly, cycle home as fast as I could, wash and change and catch a bus to Bromsgrove in time to walk to college for the seven o'clock class. By the time I had sat through a two hour lecture or practical, bussed back to Redditch and walked up the hill to home I was grateful for my supper of cheese and biscuits and a hot water bottle in bed. The following June I re-sat and passed these two subjects but how I wish I had tried harder at school.

Not only did I have to adjust to physical work and evening classes but I was also excused work on Wednesdays to go to day-release classes in agriculture.

Visiting lecturers came from Worcestershire Farm Institute to teach a wide range of subjects including animal husbandry and farm machinery, crop husbandry and animal health, over a two year course. I was the only girl amongst about a dozen boys and this had advantages as well as disadvantages.

Most of them were farmer's sons, some were farm workers who could not be spared for a full-time course and a few, like me, were farm pupils. I had always liked the freedom of male behaviour and company, their liberal approach and uncompromising attitudes and talk. However, here I was torn between two extremes. I could cuss and act tough and be accepted without special treatment, but on the other hand I was surprised to find that I could also cause embarrassment and shyness amongst the boys. I was seen as a sex object. Never expecting this in my hope of equality and mucking in with the lads it was a shock when they competed with each other to engage me in conversation or ask me for a date. My hair was cut short and was far from stylish although I bleached it with Hiltone to give it the one-shade-lighter look. I did not wear makeup to go to day release classes and whenever I could I would wear jeans.

The classes were held in a college annexe very near our house and in an effort to keep them all happy I would invite five or six of them back for coffee and biscuits when class ended at four o'clock. We would cram into the dining room and sit round the refectory table and joke around for a while. Then it was chuck-out time and I would wash up before Mum arrived home from work. I clearly flourished on it because in a combination of ongoing assessment and year end examinations I was awarded a prize for the student with top marks. Much to the disappointment of about a dozen boys!

When I attended my interview at Seale Hayne Agricultural College I had been told that I must keep a farm diary. It would have to include maps of the farm and details of the cultivation of all the crops, the fertilisers and harvest, and the animal husbandry. I took enormous pride in my diary. I had traced a large map from the library, of the scale 25inches:1mile. I outlined the farm boundary in red and showed the acreage of each field together with the rotation of crops for the current and preceding two years. In a separate section I detailed fertiliser applications and crop yields. When I worked with the herd of pedigree Friesian cattle I recorded all the dairy processes, the calf rearing and bull rearing. I followed the same format when working in the pig unit. I used my artistic skill with the illustrations, maps and information tables. Every week I brought it up to date, copying the notes that I had made every time I had an opportunity.

I had not been at Brockhill Farm for many weeks before I realised that I would be expected to drive a tractor. It was legal to drive a tractor at age sixteen and you could go on the road if you showed 'L' plates. I applied for a provisional license and looked forward to learning this new skill. I did not feel so confident when faced with reality. The tractor towered above me and I climbed up feeling very vulnerable. I was shown the basics and expected to get on with it. I had some difficulty with the wide double brake pedals, one for each side, and the hand-operated throttle needed a steady action. Within weeks I could drive smoothly and hitch the trailer and reverse it into the cowshed. During the year I learnt to operate the muck spreader, fertiliser spinner and fore-end loader, and to use the hay rake and tedder. I could hitch up and pull the four wheel trailer for bale carting but my favourite jobs were rolling the newly emerged grass or harrowing the fields. I could sit on the tractor for hours driving up and down in beautiful straight rows or turn in ever decreasing squares, making wonderful patterns in the field which would last for weeks. The acreage of some of the fields was so great that I would work in some for days on end.

Brockhill was a traditional, labour intensive farm. The pedigree herd of cattle was renowned for producing high yielding cows. I got to know all the cows by name, recognising them from the patterns of their black and white markings. I helped record the milk yields and the days on which they were ready for mating. I learnt about the cultivation of grass for pasture, hay and silage. I helped mow the fields then turn the swathes by hand with a pitchfork once the morning sun had dried the dew. The heifer calves were reared as dairy herd replacements and the best of the bull calves were reared as stock bulls, some to keep, some to sell on. The remaining bull calves were castrated, and fattened up for a few months then sold as store cattle. I helped with every process but inevitably it was the farm pupil's job to muck out the calf houses at the end of winter. The muck was so deep there was hardly enough head room to stand up and the back aching job took many days with just a fork and wheelbarrow.

Each day I would move the electric fence across a field as the cows cropped more grass. They grazed on kale in winter and hay too. It was good to fluff up the wedges of sweet smelling hay that I had helped to make.

I went out with Old George, stone picking in huge fields, collecting stones in a bucket so they would not damage the blades of farm machinery. Some winter's days we would go fencing, digging deep holes for the wooden posts then back-filling them from the piles of stones we had left at the edges of the field. We strained the strands of barbed wire across from post to post and secured it with a staple. Old George never trusted me to wield the heavy hammer while he was holding anything. We would clear out ditches and ponds and cut nettles from under hedge bottoms.

Spring followed winter and the optimism of a new season would give us energy to drill the barley and top dress the grass seeds with fertiliser.

I loved my job but there was one big problem. I did not get paid for it. I would work about forty eight hours a week alongside the men, but I was designated a pupil. I was learning my craft, not an employee. On Saturday mornings when Mr. Beckett brought round the shoe box of brown pay packets I would feel that I had earned one too.

When he came to where I was working he would ask,

'Everything alright Angela? Had a good week?'

He fished in the breast pocket of his jacket and brought out a ten shilling note for me. However, sometimes he would give me a box of chocolates instead and I would feel cheated. Over the year my pocket money from the boss increased to £2 a week.

My confidence at work was growing. I no longer felt like the new girl. I had added a trilby hat to my outfit and pushed a pheasant feather into the green hatband.

During this year I learnt the facts of life quickly. Most of the farm workers would try it on and try for a quick grope whenever they could. I was used to jokes loaded with innuendo and working with animals meant that the nitty-gritty of mating and giving birth was taken for granted.

Boys were never in short supply what with day-release classes and Young Farmer's Club. Dates for walks, the cinema or dances were plentiful. At YFC I admired one particular boy for his accomplished ballroom dancing and we thought we cut a dash skimming round the parquet floors of most of the village halls in the county. Sometimes instead of a conventional three piece band we would have a trad jazz band and skip jive or swing to the raw music.

Once, following a dance, Malcolm drove me home. As we passed a lay-by we exchanged glances and without uttering a word he brought the car to a standstill, slammed it into reverse gear and eased the car back, alongside the heaps of gravel. The car slushed in the muddy ruts but we could not care less.

The evening had gone well. We had danced together most of the time, arching our bodies and swaying to the music. The quickstep was our favourite, we were both good and loved to partner each other. Malcolm had offered me a lift from the isolated village hall and when the band had packed away I called goodbye the friends who had brought me and climbed into Malcolm's car.

Now in the lay-by the engine was off and without hesitation we leant towards each other and exchanged a tentative kiss.

'Oh, damn this hand brake, let's get in the back!'

It did not take long to loosen shirt buttons and bra straps and soon we were kissing passionately. Then the alarm bells rang and it was evident that one thing might lead to another, so, almost by tacit agreement we cooled it down and decided to go home. We had lost track of the time and it was only when we drove back in to town past the Co-op we noticed the clock and it was almost two o'clock.

As we turned into South Street we saw the lights blazing at home. My parents had been waiting for me and had heard the car. Dad rushed out of the gate onto the pavement and thundered,

'Where the hell have you been? Another five minutes and we were going to ring the police!'

Malcolm wound the window down to reply and Dad reached in and grasped him by the collar almost dragging him out through the window. Mum had come out now and she restrained Dad and was trying to usher me into the house.

'Get inside at once, we'll talk in there.'

Dad released Malcolm, turned on his heel and tried to give me swipe as he caught me up. After half an hour of warnings and questions, tantrums and tears we all went to bed. I would not be trusted to go out unless I promised to be back by midnight, so in future I often missed the last waltz, and so did my partner.

My time at Brockhill Farm was up after a year. I had worked alongside the men without any preferential treatment and I felt that my initiation period was over. I had learnt the hard way on a traditional, labour intensive farm. I had to find another place to complete my training and as the harvest was gathered in I cast about for a different sort of local farm.

Chapter 8

⟨◌⟩ Pastures new ⟨◌⟩

The name 'A. B. Quinney' was impressed into the glass of our milk bottles and I knew the large, impressive Oak Farm at Sambourne, not far from Studley. There were sister farms too; Eastern Hill at Astwood Bank and Woodrow in the green belt between Redditch and Studley.

I applied for a job and it was agreed that I could work at Woodrow with one proviso. Because they were well staffed I would not be needed full-time over the winter months. David Quinney asked if I could ride.

'Right then, I'd like you to look after my thoroughbred hunter, exercise him for two or three hours a day, and do all the stable work. He's an ex-steeplechaser and really goes. Think you can handle it? We keep my wife's Welsh cob in during the winter but the children's ponies are in the paddock.'

Of course I was over the moon. My own little empire; the stable block. Outside was a forecourt of cobbled stones and once inside the solid building of mellow red brick the floor was paved with blue bricks criss-crossed with grooves to provide a non-slip surface. There were four loose boxes, a feed room, a tack room and a hay loft over the top. I took such pride in keeping the yard and stables spotless, with never a wisp of straw out of place. The tack room smelt of saddle soap and neatsfoot oil and the supple bridles hung from their pegs above the burnished saddles on their racks.

Most days Mrs Quinney would ride her horse, Brock, and I would tack him up and lead him out ready for her. Every day, unless it was a hunting day, I would take the boss's huge, powerful gelding out for several hours across fields, through woods and down lanes. It was all countryside I knew from my earlier riding lessons. I had to choose my route quite carefully and go in a wide circle. If I turned the horse for home when we were on grass he thought he was racing again and would set off at a hair-raising gallop.

One day I helped to tack-up Brock for the trap and went with Mrs Quinney to visit her friend Lady Hertford at Ragley Hall. Once we were on a peaceful section of road I was allowed to take the reins and rather nervously drove the pony and trap for half a mile.

During the winter months I would help with the milking morning and evening but in the spring once the horses were turned out I worked on the farm full time. They had every conceivable piece of machinery for any job. The farm was managed by Charles but my closest colleague and my hero was Cecil.

Cecil: an unlikely name for an unlikely hero. He was a middle-aged herdsman on a middle sized farm. He was my minder when I was still a vulnerable seventeen-year-old.

Once again I was the only female in the workforce of about eight men, and I needed Cecil. I needed help fending off the unwelcome attentions of any bloke who thought they were in with a chance behind the hayrick; I needed help when, not to be outdone, I tossed huge bales alongside the men and carried sacks of grain from trailer to barn.

So, Cecil kept an eye on me. He understood that although I was a girl I didn't want any concessions. I had never wanted that. But there was a price to pay. I would work until I was exhausted and still keep going on. Cecil noticed, he could see the signs.

'That girl's done enough now, Charles,' he would say sharply to the manager. 'You shouldn't work her like that.'

I was faintly embarrassed but usually grateful.

I admired Cecil. I liked his lifestyle, his attitude. I could see the nice way he spoke to his wife, how he loved his children. He had a strong work ethic, something I had admired all my life. Yet anyone would have passed him off as a down-at-heel country yokel.

He was tall and gangly. He loped along, his free-ranging body moving easily. His features showed a passing resemblance to Jack Nicolson in one of his manic roles. Cecil's hair thinned above his high brow. His nose had been broken more than once when he had taken a swing at someone and come off worse. He was not a pugilist at heart but would defend his beliefs and in his younger days would put his fist where his mouth was – or where his protagonist's was.

Years of outdoor life had browned his face and forearms and his nose constantly peeled, with sunburn in the summer and cold exposure in the winter.

Cecil taught me a different approach. He was intuitive with cows and showed me how to recognise when they were off colour. He showed me how to use a shovel and broom, one in each hand. He instructed me in jobs as varied as hedge cutting to telling when a cow was on heat, of gently teaching a calf to drink from a bucket to squeezing out warble fly grubs from under the skin of cattle.

Oh, how I admired these skills and wanted desperately to learn. What better teacher than Cecil? Forthcoming with praise, gentle with criticism, sharp with warnings about safety, but oh, his humour. He would have us rolling in the gutters of the cowshed. He would sing too, especially when his throat had been lubricated with a glug from a bottle of cold cocoa. He would do songs from the shows and encourage me to make it a duet. We would sing 'I can't dance, don't ask me', and 'I hear music when there's no-one there'.

During my year at Woodrow Farm Cecil tried his hand at a spot of match-making.

'Can't you do something to cheer Ivor up?' he would say, nodding in the direction of the tractor shed. 'He's so slow he'll catch cold. Can't you two get it together?'

Now Ivor was a sandy haired, fresh complexioned, strong tractor driver but I was not sure about his sex-appeal. However I was always ready to enlarge my circle of friends and somehow I managed to get invited to tea with Ivor at his sister's house in The Grove, Studley. I soon fitted in with this warm family and became a regular visitor. Some afternoons Ivor and I would walk across the fields, leaping over brooks and climbing over stiles. Cecil was right: he was slow. Eventually by dint of bumping into him we did finally hold hands and kept them held while we walked up hill towards Studley church but mainly our friendship was on the level of banter and 'pass the cake, please' at family tea parties.

Part of my pre college training required a stint in a manufacturing dairy and after twelve months I left Woodrow to work in the milk bottling plant and laboratory at Oak Farm, Sambourne. It made an interesting change and it was quite nice to wear a white overall for six weeks instead of mucky jeans and wellingtons.

While working here I was pursued by a young man who worked on the bottle-capping machine. His name was Joseph and he was from Hungary. His family had come to England following the Hungarian revolution in 1956. He was very attentive towards me but somehow things never quite clicked as far as I was concerned. His keenness was never in doubt and he bought me gift after gift. First it was a dressing table set comprising comb, brush and mirror with a pretty design on the back. Then as he got more serious he presented me with a gold crucifix and chain. He was a catholic and this gift reflected his serious intentions. When we had been dating for a few months he asked me to marry him. I was astounded. I had never felt strongly about him. I felt I would have to let him down gently so as not to hurt his feelings. I said marriage would be impossible as I was a Methodist, almost as far from Catholicism as you could get. He began to come to church with me, even wanting to take Holy Communion. He tried to understand the beliefs of the Methodist church and desperately made all the compromises he could. In return he wanted me to go to services at Mount Carmel church and learn to acknowledge the Catholic faith.

It was time to be firmer and luckily my impending move away from Redditch combined with some direct talking from me freed me from this relationship.

During this year I had continued my ballroom dancing classes and increased my range of dances to include the slow foxtrot and tango. I decided to try for a medal and in February 1962 I achieved a bronze medal followed by a silver one in July when I had learnt even fancier footwork and a greater confidence. It was not just strictly ballroom that I loved. The Twist was the dance of the moment and I had it off to a fine art, my whole body twisting energetically from side to side. Hips locking from left to right, arms frantically keeping time. I could lift up alternate feet, not missing a beat. My shoes were always at the menders with the ball of my foot worn almost through the sole!

Soon after, the Shake took off. I sewed fringes onto my dance dresses to maximise the impact of the frenzied movement this dance required. The other dancers would stop to watch!

Once I had entered the world of work I had realised that there were gaping inadequacies in my knowledge. School had taken me so far, moralistic discussion groups a little further, but now I wanted to develop my own values and opinions.

My parents were staunchly Conservative and I began to challenge this without really knowing what politics were all about. I was surprised that my father had accepted these doctrines because he was a free thinker and had kindled within me an affinity with the underdog. I soon became aware that politics were linked with class and as my parents took on the values of the middle classes so they thought it necessary to aspire also to the creed of conservatism.

I had begun to read a wider range of fiction and had discovered English classic literature of the nineteenth century. I soon realised that these books were riddled with class values and I became aware of how people and events could be manipulated. From these fictional beginnings I developed an interest in social history from the middle ages to the twentieth century. I made slow progress. There was so much to learn. I did not want to be bigoted and needed a broader base of consciousness. I enlarged my library to include books on sociology, history and architecture. I avidly extended my knowledge of the natural sciences to include geology and astronomy. To balance this I read poetry and folk lore.

I knew I could not keep it up. Something had to give. There were not enough hours in the day. I went to dancing class, Young Farmers and had a myriad of commitments to the church. All this was in addition to hard physical work and academic study. I had to put my new found interests on the back burner for a while.

As usual family life was never static. My brother Jim and his fiancée Ann were married in 1960. I felt very sophisticated in my long bridesmaid's dress of turquoise blue brocade and loved the silver and marcasite cross and chain I had been given as a present.

Rose and Maurice had a son in 1958 and had come back to live with us. However, as soon as they could they bought their own house and in rapid succession had two daughters.

Steve, who attended Lodge Farm School, gave my parents many anxieties. He was often in trouble. He loved all the pursuits of young boys then. These included shooting stones in his catapult, playing street cricket, fighting and racing round the streets on his bike. On waste ground behind the college annexe in South Street, my friends and I had years ago built a dirt track where we could ride our bikes. It had swooping slopes and tight corners, hummocky mounds and muddy puddles. Steve and his mates had taken this over and would spend hours perfecting their techniques on their heavy framed standard BSA push bikes.

Mum was now working in the cost office at Terry's spring factory and had developed a real flair for figures. Dad had moved to the British Aluminium Company in Studley Road but still worked very long hours.

After working for two years on farms my pre-college practical training was complete. I prepared myself for leaving home. I was ready to go. Home was feeling claustrophobic. Praise had rarely been forthcoming and overt affection was not conspicuous. I knew that my parents had made gigantic sacrifices for me but was it conditional? What did they really think of me? Did they like me? I had desperately sought approval but my feeling was that they may have been disappointed in me. It was definitely time to leave Redditch behind and I knew it would never be my full time home again.

Me in the garden at South Street April 1962.

Chapter 9

∽ The bubble bursts ∽

Ifroze. The question bounced round my head and in my unconscious there stirred other unanswered and unasked questions. Questions I had thought of over the last couple of years, yet never voiced.

I had tried to unravel some inconsistencies in our family and now I was being forced to come up with the answers. I did not know the answers and did not want to face up to the unknown. Something had prevented me from pursuing any inquiries about whatever it was that I was not supposed to know. Now, just as I was settling down at college, this had cropped up.

I had moved down to Devon in October 1962 to begin the course for the College Diploma in the Science and Practice of Dairying. College life was so regimented that in today's attitude of liberalism and please-yourself it seemed like a strict training camp.

My parents had driven me down with a trunk and suitcase of not only clothes, books and a few personal possessions but items off the college list of essentials: two sets of bed linen, clearly labelled, two white laboratory coats, two dairy overalls, Wellington boots and strong shoes. I had bought a navy blue duffle coat from a government surplus store, an authentic one with wooden toggles, not a fashion design with fake cow horn buttons. I sported a CND badge on it and soon completed my student image with my long college scarf, personalised with 'Angie' embroidered in yellow chain stitch against a navy blue background.

It was with a sense of elation that I approached Newton Abbot and I used the college's map to navigate Dad to Highweek and up Mile End Road to Daracombe, the women's Hall of Residence. It was an impressive mid-nineteenth century house set in rambling gardens behind a high stone wall. The solid wooden gates were thrown open in welcome on this first day of term and the car scrunched up the gravel drive. We were greeted by the middle-aged warden who promised my parents that I would be taken care of. Once they had seen my study bedroom I wanted to settle in and get my bearings so I suggested that we should say our goodbyes and they could start for home.

My room mate was Sue Garnett whose posh accent and Hertfordshire origins seemed hardly consistent with my humble and earthy background. She was great fun and we established an immediate friendship. We chose which bed, desk and bookcase we wanted and went downstairs for the guided tour.

In small groups we were conducted round.

'This is the sitting room,' a sophisticated second year student indicated, sweeping her arm round a beautifully proportioned room which included big sofas, old fashioned arm chairs, a piano and a radiogram. On one side was a writing desk and standard lamp.

'Men are allowed to visit on Sunday afternoons only. You can make them a cup of tea if you like, but they must stay in this room.'

We trailed on past the student's dining room and the staff-only kitchen. You were not expected to eat out. Breakfast and dinner were at Daracombe Hall, lunch and tea were at college, all included in the residential fees.

Next in the tour were the boot room for wellies and wet coats and then the pantry, presumably based on a former butler's pantry. There was a stove and kettle, a huge sink and wooden draining board and an old fashioned fridge. Some chairs were set round a sturdy table.

'You can make your drinks in here. I expect you noticed there are no facilities in the bedrooms,' the authoritative voice explained. 'Leave your cocoa and coffee in the cupboard with your name on, but keep biscuits in your room.'

Outside we were whisked along flagstone paths past topiary yew trees to the tennis courts. Through the trees we caught glimpses of a beautifully tended and prolific kitchen garden protected by a stone wall up which grew espaliered fruit trees. Across the lawn were shady benches and a well positioned summer house.

'The gates are locked at 10pm. That's the curfew hour. If a boy sees you home, take care. Fanny takes her poodle for a walk just then and she doesn't miss a thing. If you know what I mean?'

For the rest of the day we settled in, arranging our books, making up our beds and unpacking our clothes.

In the morning the Michaelmas term started in earnest. We left Daracombe by the back gate and were guided along high banked lanes to college a mile or so away. Although I had attended an interview about a year ago I had not been fully aware of the beauty of the buildings and their location.

The college had a castle-like plan with a projecting room on each corner. The windows and doors were edged in pale stone against the warm red brick walls. The turrets on the corners of the keep-like structure that formed the entrance were decorated in alternate bands of light stone and brick, like streaky bacon. The flagstaff rose above the crenulated battlements.

Passing under the archway you faced the buildings ranged round a quadrangle of finely mown grass. The furthest façade was topped by a cupola. Virginia creeper just beginning to turn crimson further enhanced the appearance of this gracious building.

The college had been founded fifty years previously and we were new students in this anniversary year. It was perched on a knoll well back from the Newton Abbot to Ashburton road and looked down on the college farm and dairy buildings. The farm land extended to about three hundred acres and would provide a practical basis for lectures. From the highest points you could see Dartmoor to the north and west and the sea along the Devon coast to the south and east.

Our group was handed over to a fresh faced young man and the tour continued.

'Admin block here, each side of the main entrance and Prinny's office through that doorway. Oh, and that's the porter's lodge. He does the post for the men students, in and out. Also late passes if you want to be out after curfew. He knows what's what and who's where.' We recognised a warning note in the lowered voice.

'In the far block are the lecture theatres and laboratories, over that side the bloke's study bedrooms and over there are the dining hall and buttery.'

A cool October breeze was blowing round our stockinged legs, and my home made dress in olive green linen seemed very thin.

'Now, over to the hall. You've got the principal's talk now. Take a copy of the Internal Regulations as you go in.'

Dr. Moore talked about his high expectations of his students, academically, morally and socially. Under no circumstances were woman allowed in the men's block. Men must always wear a tie with their shirt unless in sport's kit. Women must never wear trousers. His wife had farmed all through the war wearing a skirt. He saw no reason for a common lowering of standards now.

Once we had been indoctrinated it was time for lunch. During the afternoon we were shown the dairy and farm then we trooped gratefully into the buttery for bread and butter, Victoria sponge sandwich and strong tea served in solid cups and saucers.

The daily routine was rigid. There was no freedom of choice. Attendance at lectures was compulsory and you took notes all the time, every word. It was only when I was sitting in my study copying up the barely decipherable handwriting that the meaning of the lecture became apparent.

The lectures were interspersed with practical laboratory work: dairy chemistry, botany and bacteriology. On one and a half days a week we would work in the dairy learning to make cream and butter. Over the course we produced the seven British regional cheeses using traditional methods, and several soft cheeses ranging from basic farmhouse lactic cheese to fancy French recipes inoculated with flavour producing bacteria.

Our lecturers were knowledgeable but uncompromising. The nearest we would get to familiarity would be to call them by nicknames behind their back.

I had a partial grant to help pay the fees of £100 a term for both accommodation and tuition. My parents had to top it up from their earnings and fork out an allowance for spending money.

The first big social event of the term was the Coming Up dance known to all as the Heifer Sale. The two hundred men, both first and second year, circled round the women as if they were cattle in pens being graded for size, shape and going power. There were only fifty women students so extra women were imported from the teachers training college in Exeter and from the nurses' school too. Soon after this students formed attachments and some couples stayed together all through their college life and a few went on to be married.

Friendships flourished. There was an annexe at Daracombe called the Stables. It was at the far end of the garden and not under the eagle eye of Fanny. It housed about six study bedrooms and Sue Garnett and I would often visit our friends there. There would be Pauline Bazely and Sheila Howarth, Marion and Rachel, Fishy and Perrett.

It was during one of these get-togethers over a cup of cocoa that we were telling each other about our farming experiences, home life and families. I was listing the names and ages of my brothers and sisters after briefing the group about my parents.

'Hang on,' one of them said. 'How can your oldest sister be thirty two if your mother is only forty six?'

'Um, ah, I – I'm not sure,' I stuttered, as I quickly tried to re-do the maths. 'I'll have to check that one out.'

They lost interest and began talking about someone else's family. My brain was on overdrive and long into that night I was trying to dredge up half forgotten clues to this mystery. Who could I ask? Not my parents; whatever it was all about they did not want me to know, that is why it had been a carefully guarded secret. Not Rosemary either; if she knew anything she must have colluded with my parents in the mystery. Jim was abroad on his ship, so no joy there. It would have to be Jean, the eldest, she would know.

Jean now lived in Bridport, Dorset. She had left the convent whilst she was still a novice nun without taking her final vows. My parents had told me that no reason was offered by Jean but that was typical behaviour. Although I did not ever see much of her we corresponded now and then and I felt a bond of unconventionality. I would write to her and see if I could visit.

The next time a fellow student from Dorset was going home for the weekend I scrounged a lift. The first chance I had I asked Jean about the family, and why things did not add up.

'Both Mum and Dad have been married before', she told me. 'They both had children from their previous marriages.'

I felt shocked. I had guessed there was something funny about our family but never imagined this.

'All of us children are the offspring of three different relationships,' Jean continued. Dad is my father and Jim's but my mother was not a very nice person and had affairs, and there are some other children somewhere. Your Mum is my stepmother but I call her Mum now.'

My mind was a turmoil. I couldn't take it in. Why had I not been told about it? Not been trusted?

The explanation continued.

'You have only one true brother Angie, and that's Steve. Rosemary is the child of Mum and her former husband and they managed to secure a divorce, but your Mum and Dad are not married because Dad couldn't get a divorce from my mother.'

Me, right with my sister Jean. Bridport, Autumn 1962.

I was trying hard to take in all the facts but it seemed a real muddle and I needed time to sort it out in my head. Jean told me that when Mum and Dad decided to live together and bring their three children up as one family, Mum and Rosemary had their names changed by deed poll so they all shared the same surname. This was the family I was born into.

It started to make sense. I had often wondered why there were no wedding photos, no anniversary mentioned. It was a lot to take on board. I could not think of any questions to ask my sister. I felt stupid that I did not know anything about it, and I felt hurt that I had not been trusted with the truth.

It took many years to discover any more and I gradually accepted that my parents' greatest wish was to bring us up as one united family. They had both experienced unhappy lives that they wanted to put behind them, but I looked for clues as to my own personality, and I will tell their stories now.

Chapter 10

⚭ Mum's story ⚭

As I said earlier, I had no idea until I was talking to my friends at college, that I had other than a conventional background. However, it was not until well after my father died in 1972, that Mum began to hint that she had experienced such bad times in her earlier life that it was emotionally painful and humiliating to look back at them.

Bit by bit over twenty or so years, as Mum and I have grown closer, she has recounted some of those awful times. She has often said she regretted not writing about them in a book, and I told her I would include her story as a chapter in my own book.

The good parts of her life had already been reinforced as family folk lore, but somehow they had been over shadowed by darker episodes.

Mum was born Mary Edith Winnett in March 1916, the fourth daughter of a couple who lived a tough life and always had a job to make ends meet. She tells me that she was an unplanned and unwelcome addition to the family.

Mum says her mother, my Granny Winnett, was born a lady but became a mere woman when she married. My grandmother, Maud Miriam Findon was born in 1884 at Alcester in the rural south west corner of Warwickshire.

Alcester is a small town founded on a Neolithic site by the Romans, where the Salt Way from Droitwich crossed Ryknield Street which led in turn to the Fosse Way. The River Alne joins the River Arrow on the eastern edge of town and the defensible town began between the two rivers and the trade routes. Alcester developed over the centuries and blossomed in the Middle Ages, developing into the layout still largely there today. The ancient timber framed buildings still front the long burgage plots with alleys and courts leading back from the main road.

Granny's father, James Findon, was a painter and decorator and lived in High Street, Alcester. He had been educated at the ancient Old Grammar

Mum, aged four.

School in Birch Abbey and had become a respected and well-to-do member of the artisan class. His wife Mary Ann Allcock was the daughter of a famous Alcester family, and quite a catch. They had two sons, Ernest and Albert, and three daughters: Daisy, Maud Miriam (my grandmother) and Sarah. Mary Findon died, aged twenty seven, just after giving birth to her last daughter in 1885 having borne five children in under ten years. Sarah was a feeble child, spoilt and petted by her grandparents and was slow to learn and not quite of this world.

James Findon had moved from his humble home in Malt Mill Lane to a much grander house in High Street. Widowed but with a house and five young children to care for he enlisted the help of his sister-in-law Sarah

Allcock for a number of years. Later he employed a girl from the orphanage at Ashley Down, Bristol to be his housekeeper. After a few years they were married and she became my Granny's stepmother. James Findon died in 1913, aged fifty five and the orphanage girl inherited his estate.

Meanwhile, Granny went to a fee paying 'Dame School' opposite the Town Hall. Amongst other accomplishments she learnt to dance, sing and sew. In her teenage years, having left school, she was a part time companion to Mrs. Herbert Dickson Adcock, wife of the renowned Alcester chemist. Mrs Adcock was an invalid due to a spinal injury and Granny used to read to her and help her pass the time, sometimes sitting by the window of the upstairs parlour and describing life in the High Street. When Granny could not visit, Mrs Adcock would sit on the carefully positioned chaise-longue and watch the street life reflected in a huge mirror.

Mum's father, Samuel John Winnett, was a countryman through and through. His mother, Annie, returned to her family home at Berkswell for her confinement and her son was born in 1884. She took him back to Arrow, an ancient settlement just south of Alcester and beside the River Arrow where she lived with her husband Frank, who was a farm-worker. It was the nearest village to Ragley Hall, built in 1680 and the home of the Marquess of Hertford. It was this estate that gave most of the local people their employment.

Grandad's father, Frank Winnett, born in 1861, was an agricultural labourer and together with Annie, Sam and their two later children, lived in an estate cottage on the end of a row on the main road through Arrow. Grandad went to school in Arrow and in the words of his headmistress was 'the naughtiest boy in the school and a dead-shot with a catapult.'

Later on the family - my grandfather, his two sisters and their recently widowed father moved to High Street Alcester, so it was only a matter of time before my grandparents met and began their courtship.

They married in 1907 and went to live in a nice house at the top of the Worcester Road, between Wheethly and Cookhill. The house was tied to Grandad's job and he had worked variously as a general hand, a woodsman, and finally head gamekeeper on the Ragley Estate. It was the status of this final position that had merited a nice house with many conveniences.

From what Mum tells me, it was a tough life from the start and Granny had to forget her genteel upbringing and get down to hard work straight away. Grandad had always liked his ale and was often in trouble with his ready temper and sometimes could not fulfil his duties at work. Still, with his wife to keep him on the straight and narrow path and his family responsibilities they managed reasonably well. There were rabbits and pigeons to eat as perks of the job and after a big estate shoot pheasants would be given to the keepers. They kept a pig behind the cottage and that provided much needed meat.

To increase the family income Granny would take in washing. She was a careful laundress and was asked by the Antrobus family from The Priory to do their special silk washing, their blouses and lingerie. After it was washed, then rinsed in soft rain water Granny would heat the irons in the fire and iron the beautiful, expensive garments. Finally she would place it in the wicker basket interleaved with sheets of tissue paper and Granny and one of her daughters, usually Mum, would take a handle each and walk though the wicket gate and across the fields to The Priory with the fresh, clean laundry.

By all accounts it was a disappointment to Grandad when his first three children, born at yearly intervals, were all girls; Miriam, Christina and Daisy. Grandad is described as 'happiest with a dog at his heels and a gun in his hands,' so daughters were not what he hoped for. They went to the village school at Cookhill and attended the parish church at Arrow, where they were all baptised.

By the time Mum was born in 1916 the family had left Woodland Cottage and moved over the road to a cottage on a promontory at the top of Arrow Lane. Grandad had lost his job as Head Keeper and was relegated to the rank of general estate worker and keeper. This cottage was very exposed and looked out on a wonderful view. The living room was lit by a paraffin lamp but the girls took candles to bed, promising to blow them out as soon as they were in their beds. Water was pulled up from a well down the road. They made do with two buckets a day which would be brought home on a yoke worn across the shoulders. Large amounts of water had to be heated in the copper and the clothes were boiled in the copper too. It was a large iron cauldron set into a brick structure with a brick chimney built up inside the corner of the kitchen and an opening underneath it, accessed from the back yard where you laid sticks and built a fire to heat the water.

Mum's birth coincided with quite an auspicious event. Granny Winnett was lying in bed after the birth and Mum was in the iron cot beside her. A storm was brewing, with thunder rumbling around the top of the hill where they lived. Suddenly, a bolt of lightening tore through the thatched roof, earthed on the knob of Mum's cot, and travelled down the leg through the floor boards to the pantry, where it knocked Grandad flat as he reached for the cheese dish to make his supper.

Luckily the thatch did not catch fire; Gran and the new baby survived and Grandad picked himself up and had his supper!

Mum led a Cinderella-like existence with her elder three sisters ganging up and tormenting her. By the time she was ready to start school, the youngest of the three elder girls was eleven and walked along the road with her own friends. Miriam and Chris had started at Alcester Grammar School. Granny and Grandad had a job to pay the fees, about £9 a term and Granny went out to work, doing heavy cleaning and washing. The money she earned supplemented the legacy Grandad Findon had left for his grandchildren's education.

There was no-one left for Mum to walk to school with and the family moved up into Cookhill village to one of a pair of council houses down Oak Tree Lane.

At this time Grandad was labouring as a casual worker on building sites. His pay was as unreliable as his temper. Mum has told me many tales about her childhood, and the overriding feeling is one of a great and abiding love for her mother and a fear, and sometimes a hatred, for her father. He was coarse mannered and liked his drink. Granny, and sometimes Mum, were on the receiving end of his hand, or worse still, his belt. He was almost sixty when I was born and had mellowed a little, but was still a man whose word was law. Over the years Granny had found subtle ways of dealing with his temper and he did not always have his own way.

So, Mum started the village school. She was a sensitive and artistic girl and enjoyed English and History. She wrote imaginative essays and saw romance and excitement in medieval history. It was an escape from the constraints and deprivations of home.

She won a book prize for drawing and a special commendation for music. The class regularly tuned in to the Schools Music Programme on the wireless and pupils were invited to compose and submit a piece of music. Imagine Mum's surprise when her name was called out at Prayers and everyone clapped her. She had won the competition and had her music performed on the wireless, conducted by Sir Walford Davies.

Mum was an attractive girl with fair hair and piercing blue eyes. She had inherited from the Winnetts her long face with its well defined straight nose.

She blossomed into a beautiful young woman with romantic aspirations. One day the family were seated round the table finishing their meal. The elder three girls were discussing what they hoped to achieve in their employment and asked Mum what she would like to do. Straight away she said that she would like to be a model. Quick as a flash Grandad jumped to his feet, reached across the table and slapped Mum across the face, shouting, 'You can forget that nonsense, my girl!'

Mum continued at school until she was fourteen and then it was time to start work, making a contribution to the household expenses. Before she started her first job at the famous 'Milward's Needle and Fishing Tackle Co' in lower Ipsley Street, Redditch, she needed a bicycle to travel the seven miles from home to work. Granny had saved up the down-payment and the bike was bought on the never-never with Mum calling in week by week to pay the instalments. The day of the big purchase arrived and Mum and Gran caught the bus to Redditch. The bike was bought and to save money Gran walked all the way home by the side of Mum, who was riding her new bike.

So, there they all were, at the beginning of the 1930s. Mirrie, the eldest, was working in the office at Alcester Co-operative Society in Evesham Road, Alcester and saving up to get married. Christina had joined Daye to work at Milward's and Mum was just starting. Chris and Daye as usual did not have time for Mum and used to cycle quickly ahead on the way to work and ignored her once they were there.

Milward's was a huge red-brick factory with metal framed windows and a slate roof. The main entrance was set back from the road behind iron railings and was dominated by a huge clock tower. Of course the many hundreds of people employed there, my mother and her sisters among them, entered by another door, pushing their cards into the clocking-on machine as they went down the passage in their overalls to sit at their machines or work in the warehouse packing up the goods.

Needle making was one of the industries on which nineteenth century Redditch was founded. The craft had started during the sixteenth century in London. One hundred years later it was introduced into the village of Studley, three miles from Redditch. Although many men were apprenticed to the trade it was still largely a cottage industry until about 1730 when Henry Milward saw that the industry had a big future locally. It developed in Redditch, Studley and

Alcester on a much more organised scale, with mechanisation driven by water power, speeding up the many processes in manufacture.

In 1933 the Winnett family moved from Cookhill to Alcester. They rented a terraced house in Station Road but Granny never liked it there, despite there being plenty of room for everybody.

They moved to a newly built semi-detached council house in Birmingham Road. It had a water-flushed toilet, inevitably outside, but it did have a bathroom, just off the kitchen. There was no hot water on tap, it had to be heated in the copper, and later on in the free standing, galvanised wash-boiler fuelled by gas. Granny was pleased with this house. It was on an off-shoot of the main road, a cul-de-sac down the side of the Elm-bordered Grammar School field, and ending at the ancient Ragley Mill which dated back to the thirteenth century. Granny and Grandad lived in this house until they died and whilst there enjoyed a more settled existence. Mirrie had been courted by Jim Handy, a foreman carpenter at Alcester Builders and they were married in 1931. Mum never got over not being a bridesmaid like her sisters. Mirrie and Jim lived happily at King's Coughton until in 1938 Mirrie died of septicaemia following the birth of a still-born child.

Chris continued working at Milward's until 1938 when she moved to the wages department of the Austin Aero works at Longbridge, near Birmingham. This was also the year that she met Bert Taylor at a dance. They fell for each other and became life long companions. Chris moved into lodgings at Bromsgrove in 1939, to be near him. Eventually her landlady, Mrs Poole, had to go into a nursing home and in 1940 Mum offered her sister a room in her house at Barnt Green.

Daye was married in 1933 to Fred Stanton and they went to live in a cottage at Astwood Hill on the outskirts of Astwood Bank, next to his parents and she continued to cycle to work at Milwards. When war broke out they moved to Rubery and both worked at Austin Aero works. Early the following year Fred moved away to work in a munitions factory, the house was sold and Daye moved into lodgings. Hints got back to Daye that he was having an affair but he was evidently given the benefit of the doubt because he moved back to Alcester in late 1940 and lodged with Granny and Grandad and worked at the Gauge and Tool factory.

Another family event happened during this decade. In 1934 Frank Winnett, Mum's grandfather died, and here hangs a strange tale. His wife

Annie had died in 1917 and he remarried in about 1926. His new wife was Emily Findon, the Orphan Girl who had become my Granny's stepmother. This new marriage meant that she had become Grandad's stepmother also. She outlived both her husbands to reach the old age of 93.

Mum, as the youngest, had always taken the brunt of the teasing, torments and contempt of her three elder sisters. Now, as an impressionable and emotional young woman of seventeen she had started to go out with a man who would become her husband. His family lived in Birmingham Road only a few minutes walk away. There were seven children in this large family and they occupied two adjacent cottages. He was ten years older than Mum and she admired his confidence and worldly wisdom. She enjoyed being taken out to smart places and being bought expensive presents.

In 1934 they were married and for Mum it was a case of 'out of the frying pan and into the fire'.

Until their new house at Studley was built they lived with Granny and Grandad. Mum was very excited about having her own home and could hardly wait to move in. It was beautifully furnished by them and Mum put all her artistic talent and impeccable style into practice and their home was admired by all. However, all was not well. Her new husband had a controlling personality and a bullying streak.

He liked to buy Mum new clothes, take her out and show her off, but these occasions used to end with him being violent. He hit Mum where the bruises would not show and she did not know what she had done to make her husband behave like this. She felt embarrassed and ashamed and did not confide in anyone, not even her dear mother.

In 1935 Rosemary was born and for a while everything was alright. The family moved to Cofton Hackett as Mum's husband was working at Austin Aero making plane engines. They were doing well but the bombing raids were getting too close for comfort. They moved once again to a beautiful house at Barnt Green, further away from the action.

Mum took a great pride in her house, keeping the old pieces of furniture wonderfully polished and enjoying the heritage of things passed down through the family. Mum tells me that the hall was lovely with a multi-coloured Victorian tiled floor and big oak staircase. Her innate sense of style then, as now, held her in good stead. Rosemary, aged four, started the swish fee-paying Woodrough School.

The negative side of all this was that the violence had started again and still Mum kept her batterings secret. She was torn between hoping that her husband would settle down, believing that her good behaviour and excellent house-wifely skills would save her, and giving up her home and status with shame and embarrassment. Things just were not clear cut for her.

Things finally came to a head towards the end of May 1941. It was getting near to Rosemary's sixth birthday and they had bought a puppy for her present. The puppy did a puddle and Mum's husband was furious. He started kicking the dog which began to cower and yelp. Mum could not bear to see the puppy ill-treated and intervened, trying to ward off the blows. Mum's husband hit her, punching her on the arms. Granny, who was staying there with the other guests for the party, was astounded. She took care of Mum and asked her if this had happened before. It was not long before Mum had confided the whole sorry story to her and Granny insisted on taking her daughter back to Alcester. The party broke up and Fred Stanton, Daye's husband, drove Mum and Rosemary back to Alcester with the others.

It was relief tinged with some regret for Mum. She had loved her home and when things were going well they had enjoyed some good times. They had a wide circle of friends and socialised in the local pubs. Mum took pleasure in the closeness of her special friend Irene Tatler, and another person had been admiring her from afar, James Claysmith.

Chapter 11

∽ Dad's story ∾

My father, James John William Claysmith, was born on September 20th 1905 at 4, Britannia Road, Southampton. His mother Jane was the eleventh and youngest child of James and Mary Ann Vaizey, and was born at Greenwich in 1882. James Vaizey had married Mary Ann Jones, the daughter of a greengrocer, in 1860. James and his brother George worked as barge builders in the Clapham area of London, and two of his sons (my grandmother's brothers) were also barge builders.

Dad's father James John Clay Smith was born in London, in 1876, and became a GPO telegraph linesman. My grandparents were married at Greenwich in December 1903 and moved back down to Southampton where grandfather was based. He was in at the beginning of the development of telegraphic communication, when messages were sent by Morse code and transmitted along cables. The country was criss-crossed by these lines and an enormous workforce was needed to erect the posts hewn from tree trunks and the cables linked from post to post.

There were huge strides in communication around that time, beginning in the last decade of the nineteenth century when telephone messages were largely unintelligible and not trusted by most people. Telegraphs were transmitted along wires at about twenty words a minute, and it was not until Marconi pioneered the wireless in the early 1900s that things began to develop a little more quickly.

Although the family were living in Southampton when my father was born, they had moved to Tonbridge in Kent by 1911 when another child, Mary, was born. Mary had a disability, possibly cerebral palsy, and my mother describes her crudely as being a cripple with irons on her legs.

Shortly after this my grandfather was promoted to the rank of Inspector and they moved once again, to Eastbourne. He died in 1915 of a heart attack

Dad, aged about twenty-six.

aged only thirty nine, leaving Grandma a widow with Dad aged ten and Mary aged four. Dad who by all accounts was a clever scholar won a funded place at The Blue Coat School.

In due course Grandma formed a liaison with William John Ancell who was area manager of GPO telephones in East Sussex and a man of property as well as status. However, he was already married and had a daughter called Marjorie. He was estranged from his wife but not free to marry until the criteria were finally fulfilled and then, not having heard of her for seven years she was finally presumed dead and he was able to marry.

Meanwhile William John and Grandma lived together at Southborough. Dad's stepfather did not like Dad and did not treat him well. He took him out of the Bluecoat School, aged fourteen and found him a job. Despite being area manager and in a position to give Dad a good start, he got him working as a navvy, erecting telegraph poles. This involved very hard physical labour and spending many weeks working away from home, often in a roadside hut or caravan.

Mr Ancell was jealous of Dad's good, happy relationship with his mother and was glad to keep them apart. Whenever possible Dad tried to cycle the many miles back home to see his mother, but she was prevented by her partner from making a fuss of Dad or getting up to see him back to work, when he set off at 3.30am in time for his early shift.

About this time Mr Ancell applied pressure to get the disabled Mary accepted into a residential home and so there was just Grandma, her partner William Ancell and his daughter Marjorie left in the household. Gran became pregnant and in 1918 they had a daughter, Stella. In 1924, by the time another child was due, they were able to be married and Peter was born.

By 1925 when Dad was twenty he was in lodgings at Sevenoaks in Kent. He had progressed in his job and gradually did more technical training and was doing quite well. He passed his City and guilds Technical examinations in Telephony and Magnetism and Electricity and upgraded these annually. Also by 1925 he had a full driving license. Grandma Ancell and her new family had moved to Hastings where her husband bought a fairly new, executive style house in Elphinstone Road. He owned four other houses as well and let them out for rent.

By the time Dad was twenty four he was eager to settle down but had not had much opportunity to form adult relationships. He decided to marry his step-sister Marjorie in 1929. The next August their daughter Jean May was born.

They moved to Birmingham and Dad worked at the GPO exchange in Hill Street in the city centre. At about this time it was decided to build the first automated telephone exchange at Barnt Green, south west of Birmingham and Dad became Clerk of the Works. By then he had passed examinations in electrical engineering and was a Master Electrician.

Their son James William was born in September 1934 but Marjorie was not a good housekeeper or mother and the marriage began to founder. To make matters worse over the years it was believed that she had relationships with other men and Dad began to feel very discontented with his marriage.

Due to pressure at work Dad had to move into digs at Barnt Green, living with a family of builders. By the outbreak of war Marjorie had developed a relationship with someone else and Dad asked for a divorce. She would not grant this and left the area with her lover and had two further children. Dad lost touch with her and for many years did not know her whereabouts. Jean and Jimmy aged nine and five were evacuated to Hay on Wye for the duration of the war.

Dad was living in Alvechurch now and drove up to Barnt Green to work each day. One day he gave a lift to a woman called Miss Woolf who lodged with Irene Tatler, a friend of Mum's.

Soon their stars would collide, and another chapter in my parents' lives would begin to unfold.

James had missed seeing the attractive and sociable Mary on visits to the pub with his friends. He found out what had happened to her and decided to go to Alcester. He talked things over with Mary's father who agreed that they could go out together once she had filed for divorce. They hoped she could bring a case for cruelty.

Their relationship began and whenever they could they went for walks together and long drives into the countryside. They also enjoyed socialising with their group of friends in pubs. Their relationship developed into love and James said he would like to marry Mary when they were both free.

Mum's husband, however, did not take things so slowly. Once she had moved back down to Alcester he began an affair with Mum's best friend, Irene Tatler, and she moved into his house. Later on a child was born.

Mum wanted to give Dad a token of affection for his birthday in September 1941 and she bought a car from her foreman, Harry Boycott, at the Gauge and Tool factory. She paid £5 for the little Austin Seven called 'Harriet'.

Mum tried to get a divorce using the 'weekend away' bill as a reason, but she refused to provide intimate evidence so it failed.

My parents continued seeing each other as often as they could and one day a colleague of Mum's told her there was a house to let at Astwood Bank, near Redditch and she and Dad decided to set up house together.

On November 23rd 1942 Mum, Dad and Rosemary moved into this house, and they applied to get Jean and Jimmy back from wartime evacuation in Hay on Wye.

The first Christmas at Astwood Bank was a very meagre affair. Auntie Chris and Bert helped Mum and Dad to buy a few things for the three children's stockings and some tangerines and nuts. Grandad would not let Granny visit because he was disgusted and ashamed that Mum and Dad were living together.

Mum had many difficulties looking after her step children, especially Jean. They had not been used to any parental guidance or discipline, and no one found it easy to make the bonds that were essential to form a new family.

Mum continued working at the Gauge and Tool, leaving the house at 8.30 every morning to cycle to Alcester. Every penny was needed as money was very tight. Dad's pay was £6 a week and the rent was £2-10s so with the other bills this left very little money to buy food for five people. Dad patched the family's shoes as best he could, sticking on rubber soles and heels with the shoes fixed over the iron last.

To increase his income Dad decided to do radio repairs at home as well as go to work. He did quite well at this and in the spring of next year Mum was soon able to give up work. This was a real relief to her as the long bike ride home was almost more than she could endure. Once home she would begin the chores, often continuing with the washing and cleaning right up to bedtime.

Mum's husband had requested access to his daughter, Rosemary, and Mum had reluctantly agreed, although no maintenance was ever paid. Inevitably he found out where they were all living and in February 1943 arranged to call at the house with a private detective. Mum and Dad were identified as co-habiting and Mum's divorce was set in motion. The divorce was made absolute in September and Dad had to pay £9 in costs as co-respondent.

Granny and Grandad Winnett started to visit again after this and Grandad broke his year long silence.

Mum and Dad felt that as long as they were together they could cope with anything and they were so pleased with their new home they decided to throw a big family party for Christmas 1943. Grandma Ancell and all the family came down from Yorkshire and of course Granny and Grandad Winnett were there too. On Christmas Eve Auntie Chris and Bert arrived with a Christmas tree which was duly decorated and they began to prepare all the food that everyone had contributed. All their problems were forgotten during this season of merry making, but soon it was time to pull their horns in and start counting the pennies again. They were expecting a baby and would need all the money Dad could earn.

Auntie Chris had been very kind to Mum. She had moved back to her parent's house when Mum had left her husband and was close enough to visit regularly and help out whenever she could.

Auntie Daye was divorced from her husband and had also moved back to Alcester and worked in the Golden Cross pub at Wixford. She started going out with a man called Jimmy Frost who was stationed at the nearby RAF base at Honeybourne. However she soon took a job as a secretary at the Austin Motor Company and finally married her boss.

But meanwhile, during the war years, things would be moving on, back in Hastings.

Dad's half sister Stella had married David Meaden, who was in the RAF during the war. He was posted to Doncaster in Yorkshire and Auntie Stella moved up to live with him and in 1942 their daughter Wendy was born. The bombing raids in Hastings were so bad that Grandma Ancell, now widowed once again, together with Peter decided also to move to Doncaster. Peter in his late teens fell for a Yorkshire girl and in February 1943 with Peter aged eighteen and Elsie aged nineteen got married, asking Dad to be best man. They had their first two sons, Richard and Robert and stayed in Yorkshire until the end of the war.

The house in Elphinstone Road, Hastings, had been closed down for the duration of the war but in 1945 Grandma Ancell with Stella, Peter and their respective families all moved back to live in the house again. Things did not go well, there were too many people living in the house – five adults and five children. There were constant rows and they just could not get on together.

Auntie Stella's husband David was a typesetter at the newspaper offices in Hastings and supplemented his income by driving a taxi. He did not have time to sort out the squabbles. Stella finally went to the council offices and begged for a flat. It paid off and they were allocated a big, light, three bedroomed flat in London Road. The timing was just right as they were expecting their third child.

Grandma Ancell had been left four properties by her second husband, apart from her home. Two were severely bomb damaged and she had financial reparation for those. The other two houses had tenants. As the tenants moved out she decided to sell them. She gave Peter the down payment for a house from what was, of course, his inheritance from his father. Apparently this was on the understanding that it would become his family home and he would not sell it. It must have been a relief to move his fast growing family into a home of their own.

Grandma, Auntie Stella and family continued at Elphinstone Road for a while, until that also was sold, as well as the remaining rental house, now that the tenants had left. Some of the money went towards paying off Peter and Elsie's house and some towards buying a house for Stella and David, in Braybrooke Road, Hastings, which cost £1,500, the same as Peter's.

Peter sold his house in less than a year and moved on to several bigger houses, one of which my family and I stayed in during 1949/50. Eventually in the mid 1950s Peter moved with his family up to Cumbria and worked at the Nuclear Power Station.

Mum and Dad did not have any inheritance due to them but Grandma Ancell did help them out by sending money so everyone could have a new winter overcoat.

I was born in May 1944 during a period of comparative tranquillity and affluence and took my place as the fourth child in that extended family.

Chapter 12

⚮ Back to me ⚮

It was with some difficulty that I acted normally when I went back to Redditch at the end of the college term. My sister's revelations had stunned me.

I saw my parents in a different light. Partly I admired them for going against the conventions of the day and living together, despite disapproval from some family members and the world at large. The other part of me still felt excluded from this secret. Would they ever get married? Would they want to? Would I know? There was no way that I felt I could talk to them about it. It had been covered up for twenty years so it was not going to become a topic of conversation now.

I consoled myself with the knowledge that they must love each other very much, and I now realised why I had never seen any wedding photographs.

I settled back into the routine of college and the societies that I had joined. The Pioneer Club was the gateway to several exciting activities. The two I chose were Moor Walking and Caving, as opposite as they could be.

Moor walking was exhilarating. We would tramp across the springy heather and startle sky larks on their nests; we would splosh through boggy rushes and scramble over lichen covered boulders, scattering ponies and sheep. Our destination on Dartmoor was usually one of the craggy granite tors and we would return to college drunk with fresh air and half a pint of shandy from a pub in Ashburton or Bovey Travey.

Caving was another matter entirely. It was scary. It was dark, dirty and potentially dangerous. As in the other outdoor pursuits the women would break the taboo of wearing trousers and change behind a tree when we were near the entrance to the cave. You did not want baggy clothes but you needed something that provided special protection for your elbows and knees. We wore helmets with carbide lamps. These could be tricky to adjust and needed

By the fish pond, South Street, September 1962. Me, Steve, Mum, Jim.
Dad standing at the back.

just the right amount of water to trickle over the carbide to give the gas that ignited into a flame.

After the first couple of descents and a certain amount of safety training we went deeper and further into the network of tunnels and caverns. We learnt, mainly by experience, the technique of wriggling along on our bellies, propelling ourselves by using our elbows like flippers. Within a couple of minutes we would be plastered in cold, slimy mud, but this seemed to help with slipping you through especially low tunnels, maybe only sixty centimetres high. Sometimes we would have to wade through underground streams and the experienced pot-holers would lead the way in case there was a deep sump. When we finally reached a huge cavern which often smelt, somehow, of a tomb and all beamed our helmet lamps across the roof we could see weird rock formations and stalactites. Occasionally if we were wading along a watery tunnel up to our knees in cold, red, thin mud, a huge boulder hanging down from the ceiling might block the way. The more daring members would stop at nothing and crawl on their hands and knees under a rock weighing several tons. Once in a while we had to take a deep breath and put our heads under water to crawl past obstacles.

One of the reasons I liked caving was that it was an unconventional activity and people were both impressed and horrified when I related my adventures.

Some weekends I would join the rock climbing expedition and we would make for Haytor rock with our ropes. The climbs were graded in terms of difficulty and although I never did a 'v.diff' climb there was always an adrenalin rush and a sense of relief and achievement as I made it to the top.

Potentially less exciting, but good for the soul, was my membership of the college Christian Union. This inter-denominational group did not take the form of the fervent prayer meetings and questioning bible study I had been used to. We did have some discussion groups but mainly we met up to go to church together.

As a Methodist I began by going with a few other students to the Methodist church in Tor Hill Road, Torquay but it was not long before we joined in with the college tradition for all non-conformists to link up and go to Upton Vale Baptist Church in Lymington Road. This huge building had regular congregations of over one thousand people. The U-shaped balcony rose tier above tier supported on iron pillars on the ground floor. The charismatic minister, the Rev. Stanley Voke drew crowds from far and wide. The Baptismal services were the most emotional. Church members who had found the Lord were baptised by total immersion in the huge baptismal pool revealed beneath pews at the front of the church. After the service we streamed out onto the steps feeling high with emotion and in touch with the Lord.

It seems strange that due to various events in my life, that twenty years on, I rejected the teachings and beliefs of the Christian church and now, another twenty years later, I have no belief at all. I had become a full member of the Methodist church at Easter 1962, and then I believed ardently in the doctrines of the church and tried to fulfil my responsibilities as a Christian.

Academically life at college continued without too much difficulty. I found that my two years of day release classes covered a lot of the work in the first year. We studied agricultural chemistry, bacteriology, botany and zoology as our science subjects and in addition learnt about building construction, economics, accountancy and farm machinery. Our main subject of dairying was very practical and most of the students enjoyed that. As the year progressed, the science subjects started making life a lot harder. Towards the end of the Trinity term examinations loomed up and I realised I had better start revision.

Dad tried to boost my moral with an amusing letter encouraging me by saying,

'Put your best foot forward and your shoulder to the wheel. Keep your chin up and your nose to the grindstone. Put your back to the wall and keep your head above water.'

Second year students were allowed a car and Dad promised to buy me one if I was successful in the exams. I buckled down to swotting and thankfully passed.

I had plagued my parents to allow me to live out of Hall in the second year, and they finally agreed, so before the long vacation I sorted out my new digs. I was sorry not to be lodging with my old room mate, Sue, or my best friend Marion Baker but I got fixed up with a nice room in a house in Seymour Road. My landlady was Mrs. Lloyd and her husband kept a tobacconist's shop in Newton Abbot. She was on the list of approved lodgings and had many years experience of students.

The three months of summer vacation was not a holiday. Far from it. Although I did have chance to meet up with Sylv Beard, Judy Davies, Jane Adams and the rest of the gang, I also had to go to work. I needed to increase my experience of working in a commercial dairy and had secured a job in the laboratory of The Midland Counties Dairy at Aston in Birmingham.

I travelled by train from Redditch to New Street and walked the mile and a half to arrive at the dairy at just turned eight o'clock – a special concession. The noise in the bottling plant was unbelievable: clanking, clashing glass and rattling, reverberating conveyor belts, hissing hot water and the thudding of the capping machine. The scene was dazzling. The light reflected off the bottles, the huge reels of foil for the caps, the steel of the machinery and the bright white of the overalls.

As a laboratory assistant at least there was the sanctuary of the lab to return to with the samples and swabs, but obtaining them was fraught with difficulty. I sampled the raw milk fresh in from the farms, then the pasteurised or sterilized milk from the heat processing room, and then finally, the bottled, cooled product. I took swabs of the bottles, the cap foil and the machinery.

The samples were diluted and inoculated onto plates of jelly-like growing medium or mixed with nutrient broth. I incubated them at different temperatures to see what bacteria, if any, grew and in what conditions. The work was mentally demanding and physically tiring and I looked forward to the weekends when I did not do an overtime shift. Saturday evenings usually meant a dance or a visit to the cinema.

Sylvia had started work in a bank in Birmingham after taking her 'A' level exams. She had developed new friendships in the sixth form and made new friends at work but we were still very close and saw each other regularly. Our common link was still church but our chief delight was film going.

Judy was also at work. She had joined the Civil Service and worked as a Tax Officer. At weekends I sometimes caught the 147 bus and got off at Grovelly Corner to walk to her house for the day. Sometimes we would go into Birmingham where her Mum worked at Gray's Store.

Jane Adams was also at work but we met up at dances when we could get together with the Young Farmers.

Sometimes I was allowed to drive Dad's car. He had bought an Austin Mini in early 1962. It was the first new car he had ever had but by then we did not need a big family car and in any case Mum was fed up with him spending so much time lying on the road outside, trying to mend the ancient but classy vehicles he liked. He had moved on from the grey Mk II Jaguar to an old white Chrysler convertible which we christened 'The Snow Queen'. When this vehicle finally clapped out his next purchase was an Allard. It looked very stylish with its wide chrome bumper, big square radiator grille, huge, bulging wheel arches and long bonnet. He felt that the Mini was something of a come-down but could see the sense of it. Luckily I had learnt to drive in a Mini and passed my test in July 1961, ten weeks after getting my provisional license, so I felt confident in this particular car. Auntie Chris and Auntie Daye had both remained loyal to the company that had employed them for so many years and also had a Mini each, made of course, at Longbridge, Birmingham.

On Saturdays I would maybe go shopping with Auntie Chris to Stratford-upon-Avon or Worcester and drive her car. She dressed very elegantly and I looked forward to the chance to wear high heels and gloves for a day.

Auntie Chris had retained her hobbies of embroidery, knitting, lampshade making and flower arranging and we would visit the Web craft shop to stock up on various materials. Occasionally we would go to Birmingham by train and call at the huge Midland Educational store. Auntie had taught me how to embroider and knit and we would choose our wool or our silks. By this time I was also quite experienced at dress making and would search the Simplicity or Butterick pattern books for new outfits to make.

With only a few weeks of the vacation left Dad said he would look for a car for me. One day when I returned home it was waiting outside. It was an old, upright, black Ford Anglia and had cost Dad £10.

'We'll take her out later, Angie, and you can give her a go,' Dad said.

After tea we took the car out down the back lanes for a drive. I was scared witless, and pulled in to a gateway. I burst into tears.

'Dad, it's no good, I can't drive it,' I sobbed. 'The seat is so worn and low I can't see out properly, and the steering wheel doesn't seem to connect with the wheels.'

I didn't like to say, but the orange flipper-type trafficators sometimes did not always work either.

'You'll soon get used to it, ducky,' Dad assured me, and I struggled to gain confidence. At least I had a car and a couple of weeks later, in early October I set off to drive to Newton Abbot for my second year at college. It took eight hours to drive the 170 miles down the A38 using my new leather covered road atlas to navigate.

The car served me well for six months. The three speed gear box had an ideal ratio for the steep hills of Devon and Dartmoor. On another trip I left many cars over-heating on the grass verge on the famous Porlock Hill in Somerset.

Finally I arrived at my new digs and unloaded my boxes. I installed myself into my small but well equipped study-bedroom overlooking the rear garden of 32, Seymour Road.

Two first-year students also lodged there: Christine Aldwinckle from Leicester and Janet Bayliss from Worcester. I could not have had nicer young women to share digs with and we all became good friends.

Chapter 13

⌘ Second year ⌘

As study at college had become tougher so social life had blossomed. I now had the freedom of a car and with petrol at four gallons for £1 even my student grant would stretch to keeping the car fuelled up.

Chris Aldwinckle had friends on Dartmoor and we would drive out to visit them at their farm at Poundsgate. Algy and Jean lived down a track far from the road and you crossed a stream to reach the farmhouse door. It must have been a tough life for them but it satisfied all my romantic notions of farming: sheep on the high moor, rounded up on horse back; bumping up the track in a Landrover, fetching the water from the spring.

Chris and I would ride the ponies sometimes and gallop across the springy turf with the wind in our hair and the ponies' manes swept back and they tossed their tails with the exhilaration.

Algy and Jean had two wonderful greyhounds, graceful and beautifully tempered. They would lounge elegantly on the rug in front of the Aga or crouch on the battered sofa. Jean and Algy seemed tireless and had the resilient nature essential for farming.

Sometimes Janet, Chris and I would pile into the car and drive into Torquay for a coffee at Macari's on The Strand, or just drive for the pleasure of it. If we had boys to take us out we would go in their car to the pubs in the surrounding villages: The Church House Inn, The Passage House, The Halfway House, The Hole in the Wall and the others frequented by students. Best of all was having a lift in a Morgan or MG or sometimes a Triumph Roadster. My old mate from Redditch, Dave Woods, had a Morgan three-wheeler and I had developed a taste for sports cars from the times we used to knock around together and drive along the lanes of Worcestershire. I had always fancied a sports car, who wouldn't? I scoured the pages of The Exchange and Mart magazine hoping that one

The lady students, National Diploma in Dairying Seale Hayne
Agricultural College 1963. Me, front row, left.

day I may afford the £150 needed to buy a Morgan and wave goodbye to my upright Anglia.

My car was named Emma, which was a college expletive for when swearing was not appropriate. I needed to swear at her quite often.

My friend Marion Baker came from Cheriton Bishop, a village to the west of Exeter. Some weekends we would drive in Emma out to visit her home where her father worked on a farm. During one of these visits she introduced me to a boy who worked on a neighbouring farm and we were immediately attracted to each other. His name was John Kift and he had long, curly, dark hair and a high forehead. I thought he looked like a young Jimmy Stewart. We wrote or rang each other regularly and I was inspired to write soppy poetry about him.

I looked forward to the times he would ride down on his motor bike to visit me and I would ride pillion as we burnt up the miles of the Devon lanes.

Until then I rather thought that the swinging sixties had passed me by but with John wearing his leathers and me in black stockings and mini skirt I felt quite Bohemian. We would stop at coffee bars and listen to Elvis on the juke box while our steaming mugs of coffee cooled on the Formica topped tables. I would be frozen to the bones but it would be worth it. The motor bike would be parked on its stand outside, shining black with its emblem picked out in gold. I would look across the room to the juke box where John was punching out the numbers for his selection of records. Yes, he was handsome. His slim hips looked their best in his black and white tapered trousers. The sinewy legs were accentuated by the silver buttons sewn down the outer seams.

'Your coffee is getting cold,' I would call. 'Come on.'

I would blow the froth to the side of my cup and sip it, thinking of the ride of a lifetime I had just experienced. I had looked over his shoulder and seen the speedo reach eighty five and knew instinctively that this was not the top speed. I had clutched John tight, for warmth, not fear. The smell of his leather jacket had been comforting.

But John was shy and our meetings were not frequent enough for our relationship to develop quickly. It took about six months to reach the hand-holding stage!

As the academic year progressed so our subjects became more detailed. I discovered to my surprise that I enjoyed the science subjects; botany, microbiology and zoology especially, dairy chemistry to a lesser extent.

Previously I had assumed that with my interest in practical farming and dairy husbandry that I would aim to become a herdswoman, but with my newly developed interest in the sciences fresh horizons opened up. I desperately wanted to work in Africa for Voluntary Service Overseas. This work involved setting up new agricultural projects and training the staff. The contracts lasted a year and the pay was very basic and little more than subsistence level. I had a preliminary interview at college and was accepted for a proper interview in London. At this stage I told my parents about it and they refused to give their consent. I was told that great sacrifices had been made to give me a good education and I was not going to waste it by working abroad. I could read between the lines and knew what they meant.

I was devastated that I could not take up this opportunity. It combined travel with a very interesting job. I felt, rather patronizingly I'm ashamed to say, that it fulfilled my Christian social commitment. However, my parents were not to be swayed and I was told to look for work in the UK.

I could consider a career in the Ministry of Agriculture, Fisheries and Food, work in a dairy lab, do research or even teach Rural Science if I wanted to add a year at teacher's training college to my studying. By March of the second year we were encouraged to make career decisions and begin applying for jobs. The leading companies such as Fison's, United Dairies, Cadbury and BOCM held interview sessions at the college.

My mother strongly encouraged me to try for a job at Cadbury's dairy at Bournville on the outskirts of Birmingham. I knew that if I did this I would be expected to live at home and commute to work. I don't think Mum could understand why I was so against this. She had always been, and still is a controlling parent and was reluctant to let me spread my wings and leave the nest. It was many years before I was forgiven for not following up this option for employment and it was lumped together with a previous sin. This was not applying for Studley Ladies Agricultural College, once again with the chance of continuing to live at home. I was told I was selfish to take, take, take for years and then clear off to live miles away. I remembered the scene vividly.

'There is no reason for it,' my mother had hissed. 'No reason at all. After all we've done for you, made sacrifices, educated you. I've stood there in that porch, stripping off your cow-muck clothes and passing your warm dressing gown. This is how you repay us. There was a college just a few miles away at Studley. You could have gone there, but you wouldn't. What could your reason have been? Why? I ask you again, why?'

I had drawn in a breath, trying to form an answer but the tirade continued.

'Why did you choose to leave home and go to a college over one hundred miles away? Do you hate it so much here? We're here to support you, look after you. Do you think I've done all this for you so you can give up your home and family when you could be living here still with me and Daddy? It's beyond me. There can't be a reason for it.'

By then I was in tears, tired of trying to butt in, put my own opinion, answer the questions being hurled at me. I made another attempt to stammer the words out,

'Well Mum, it's like this. I'm eighteen now. I want to do things for myself. Try things out.'

Her scream ripped through my reply.

'What things? Drugs, do you mean?'

Love, approval, education: they were all conditional. After a lifetime of seeking approval, and notching up achievement after achievement, if maybe in only small ways, I have never felt parental approval. After sixty years of hoping to gain it, my mother recently told me that she did not ever praise me in case I became big-headed.

I decided to apply for a laboratory job with United Dairies who had dairies all over the south west of England. The choice was wide; they had cheese factories, dried milk plants, evaporated milk creameries, huge bottling plants and clotted cream dairies. The milk-rich dairy counties of Devon, Dorset, Somerset and Wiltshire abounded in these factories. Step one was to succeed in the first round of interviews held at college, the choice of dairy could be made later. At least half of the second year dairy students applied and out of these dozen about eight were accepted.

Next came the choice of where to go. It was not just the product, there were geographical considerations. I wanted to be far enough away from home to minimize interference but not so far that it was inconvenient to visit if I wanted to. This would take some thinking about, meanwhile there were other developments in my social life.

The Folk Club was held weekly at The Ship Inn in the lee of the clock tower at Newton Abbot. Whenever I was not writing up lecture notes, reading through text books for key phrases for an essay or swotting for exams I would join a group of fellow students and meet at the bar of the pub ready for an evening of traditional folk songs. There was no pressure to sing or play a tune, or even join in on a chorus unless you wanted to. It was a relaxing background to a pint. I had been going for two or three weeks and rather fancied a blond-haired student, Dave Addis.

One session, a couple of weeks before the end of the Lent term, I was jostling for a better view of a performer when suddenly I realised someone was looking at me. I flicked my eyes left and right and saw a pair of deep set, intense, green eyes looking right into my soul. My knees buckled slightly and after returning the gaze for two seconds I looked away. Focusing on the band, with no interest at all, I conjured up the image of the face I had just seen. Thick, dark brown hair crinkled into tight curls, and long sideboards, gingery coloured, framed a handsome face with high cheekbones. A rather winsome expression had hovered round the eyes and mouth. Should I risk another look? Yes! There, I'd done it, and he was looking at me again. His mouth broke into a tentative smile and then I noticed the little pointed beard giving him a rather arty look.

The band had played their last number, the set was over and Dave and the other blokes crowded round me to arrange lifts home. I searched the thinning crowd but my mystery man had gone.

Needless to say it took no second invitation to join the gang for another visit next week. I had pictured a certain face all week and I was not disappointed when he appeared at the bar to buy half a pint of best bitter. We cast each other a few glances in the first half and could hardly wait for shoals of herring to be caught and gypsies to finish roving. In the interval he pushed through the crowd and asked if I would like a drink. I stood beside him hardly daring to move, feeling tingly electric shocks travelling down my spine. There wasn't much chance for conversation once people had started to sing or play in the second half. I was going to need patience. This man was shy. When the music finally stopped and last orders had been bought I just had chance to say I was a student and would be going home at the weekend for a four week vacation. He had a bus to catch and I was re-absorbed by my group of friends.

I left college on Friday hoping that I would see him again, sometime in the future. I would not be back in Newton Abbot until the third week in April and before then I had my holiday job to get to grips with.

My journey back to Redditch in my car, Emma, was rather traumatic. I fulfilled a long standing arrangement to visit John Kift still living and working on a farm west of Exeter. We spent a very pleasant day together which included going for a walk and picking a bunch of beautiful wild flowers. The time came for me to leave and if truth be told I wondered if I would see him again. I drove home feeling rather unsure and as I passed through Tewkesbury I made a wrong turn. I knew the town quite well and realised if I turned right up the Bredon road I could correct my mistake in a few miles. Before turning I positioned the car correctly, checked the road back and front and began to turn. Wham! I was suddenly hit squarely on the left of the car as I drove across the other lane. The other car had shot far too fast over the slightly humped river bridge just down the road. Emma's radiator was smashed and leaking, the left headlight broken and the steering did not work. Someone helped me push it to the side of the road and then I phoned Dad.

While I was waiting for him I stood my bunch of flowers on Emma's radiator. I guessed that this would be the end of the road for her. I was right. Once Dad was there he arranged for a nearby garage to take her as scrap and had to give the mechanic a fiver to haul her away.

Dad drove me gently back to Redditch in his Mini realising I was very shocked and also very disappointed. I did not own another car for five years.

The following Monday I began my vacation work. The job I had arranged was at a chair factory. Not the comfy upholstered sort with a pretty fabric cover. These were garden chairs, fishing stools and camping seats. The factory consisted of three sections but I only got to work in two of them. The brightly striped nylon fabric was stitched into shape with narrow channels down the sides. This stitching, and the cutting out was done by more mature ladies in a separate room that was clean, warm and had a radio playing. The piles of seats and backs would arrive on trolleys and be shunted into place beside the appropriate machine.

The first job I was allowed to do was to operate the bending machine. A rack of aluminium tubes, cut to length, stood ready and I had to place them into a jig and bear down on a foot pedal and the press would bend the tubes to shape, forming right angles at the appropriate place. By lunch time I wondered why on earth I had chosen such a tedious, mindless job. I was isolated from the other workers, had no radio, and was bored out of my skull. The next three days were spent perfecting this limited skill. This involved bending my back as little as possible, swopping legs to avoid cramp and thinking about something else.

The drilling machine came next. Requiring a little more concentration, I had to drill holes in the metal tubes at the exact marks ready for bolting the chairs together. A week of this and I was deemed to be ready for the assembly line.

The conveyor belt moved very slowly. Each of the operatives did their particular job and replaced the part-assembled chair back on the belt. I had made no friends among the work force and communication was non existent. Four of us stood on each side. Firstly the back sling was threaded on to the frame and the seat was added to another bit. The various bits of metal would be held together and a bolt pushed through the holes. The electric tools hung on slings across the conveyor and I would reach over and grab the handle and tighten the bolt heads. Finally, and most boring of all, was inserting the plastic caps into the ends of the tubes.

The days dragged on and on and I longed for a more demanding challenge. In an attempt at being pally I tried joking with the young women. We didn't seem on the same wavelength. One day when I thought we could have done the job more efficiently, I called across the assembly room,

'Come on, speed up you slow moo!'

All hell broke loose. A torrent of abuse was directed at me, chairs piled up on the conveyor belt, the women joined ranks in a defensive group and the foreman appeared from his office.

My terminology had not been appropriate. At agricultural college that phrase would be a mild joke. Anyway, Alf Garnett used it! There was real swearing for when the situation demanded it. We were both taken into the office to account for our behaviour. Unknown to me, the other woman was a trouble maker, known for her quick temper. I was a new girl and did not know the ropes. I only had another week to go so a stern warning put me in my place and eventually normal service was resumed.

Was I glad to finish at that factory? My spending money for my last term at college was earned and with relief I prepared to travel by train back down to Newton Abbot.

Chapter 14

⊙ Bohemia and academia ⊙

inals in seven weeks. The thought filled most of the students with dread. Essays to finish, practical tests to get through, not just laboratory work but dairying too. We had to complete our schedule of manufacturing processes and be marked on our efforts. Cream, butter and cheeses to make, all under the eagle eye of Miss Darbyshire. When these ordeals were over we had the written papers, taken in the Great Hall under strict examination conditions. Interspersed with these were the things that caused almost all the students to tremble with nerves: the oral exams. There was no opportunity to waffle, padding out your answers with irrelevancies, you were asked direct questions, face to face, and you had to think of something intelligent to say. Until then, I had six more weeks of study.

I had other things on my mind: Folk Club. I had been thinking of the handsome man I had briefly met last term and hoped there may be chance to speak to him again – if he was there. On Monday I was in the low-ceilinged back room of the pub, eyes scanning the group of folkies. Oh! I could see him, tall and slim-hipped, wearing a black polo neck jumper under his donkey jacket.

I tried to look nonchalant but I was anything but cool inside. He eased over to me before the first singer launched into 'The Jug of Punch'.

'Want a drink?' he questioned.

I looked at his half pint glass and judged that this was his standard drink.

'Yes please, half of shandy.'

The music had begun and there was no chance for conversation but in the interval he said,

'Would you like to go to the cinema in Torquay at the weekend?' His deep voice was as soft as Devon butter.

'That would be good,' I gasped, not hearing or caring what film was mentioned.

Bryn 1964.

On Saturday evening he met my bus and we walked to the Odeon in Abbey Road. He told me he was a printer and had done his apprenticeship at Bendles' in Torquay, although he now worked in Teignmouth. I drank in the details wondering how much of my own life to reveal.

Later, hurrying for the last bus, we talked about the film, its director and the acting. We arranged to meet up on Wednesday for a walk in Newton Abbot. I hopped up onto the number twelve bus and turned round to say goodbye as the bus pulled away.

'By the way, what's your name?' I called.

'Bryn!' he shouted back.

I managed to struggle through the next four days. It was a case of having to, college work demanded it, but Wednesday evening saw me dressed in my slim, black and white hound's tooth check skirt, thick black stockings and black polo neck, ready to meet Bryn.

We walked and walked round Newton Abbot exchanging family details, interests and opinions. I liked him. I liked him a lot. He represented the artistic side of me, the side I had given up to study agriculture. I had always felt that to be labelled 'unconventional' was a compliment and here it seemed, was a kindred spirit.

Bryn told me he liked to paint and shared a studio with Mike Tolliday. He had been to Paris twice to look round the French art galleries. He had stayed in a tiny hotel near the Left Bank and had spent the days tramping the streets and soaking up the atmosphere.

He read poetry and especially enjoyed the Beat Poets; Jack Kerouac, Allen Ginsberg and Lawrence Ferlinghetti. The rebellious and charismatic Dylan Thomas was another favourite. He asked what I read and wondered if I knew the work of William Burroughs or John Steinbeck. The last name struck a chord. At least we had something in common.

I listened to him talking with enthusiasm about cinema, the film society he went to, directors, locations, actors. Although in essence he was polite, gentle and shy he was knowledgeable and articulate about all the arts. A newly coined label clicked into my mind. He was a beatnik. He was a product of the new social and political consciousness that was critical of consumerism and conventionality. He believed in self expression: that was evident after just five meetings.

It was time to make my way home and Bryn walked me to the gates of number 32. He asked if I would like to go to tea on Sunday, meet his family, look at his sketch books. Somehow this seemed so natural that I had no problem accepting. He was so different to the farm boys and the red necked college students I knew. He made me feel bohemian, alive, grown up.

On Sunday Bryn met me off the bus and as soon as we were side by side on the pavement he reached across to hold my hand. I was his girl! I was caught by that old black magic!

Even the approach to his home was fascinating. After gliding on cloud nine along several streets of terraced houses and bed and breakfast establishments we turned up a wide track with a quarry directly in front of us. Leading uphill to the right of this and just wide enough for two people, a steep stony track passed between drifts of late primroses and wild cyclamen, shading under trees that became denser as we climbed, avoiding knobbly chunks of bedrock that poked through the surface of the track. After fifty yards I could see a building looming up on the hillside. It stood out starkly in white and its angular projections and flat roof proclaimed it as dating from the 1930s.

Brambles, nettles and thistles were encroaching on all sides but someone had clipped them back to reveal a narrow, rocky path up to the steep concrete steps. A hand painted sign revealed that it was called 'Stantaway House'.

We entered the building through green-painted double doors and started up the stone steps. Long windows with crinkly frosted glass lit the stairway. Bright sun shafted in and curdled the brown varnish on the handrail and doors. Bryn's parents' flat was the highest one of four and on the third floor. The green marbled lino curled in the stifling heat, as he felt for the key in the drawer of an old sideboard on the landing.

I received a warm welcome from his mother and a distant look from his rather vague father. Introductions were over and we were told tea would be ready in ten minutes. Bryn said that I could put my corduroy jacket in his room and opened a door behind the dining table.

The bedroom was about nine feet long and seven feet wide and it was absolutely jam-packed with things. Crates of records were stacked up, one on top of another on one side of the small window, a record player sat on top of a chest of drawers and beside a plywood wardrobe crouched a bookcase, spilling out volumes of every size. I then noticed a Formica topped table covered with some sort of craft work and a spidery angle poise lamp bolted to the table edge. The bed was high and underneath it I could see a portfolio and rolled up tubes of paper. Bryn grinned,

'This is it! Where it's all at! The centre of my universe.'

I mentally compared it to my carefully furnished room in Redditch, where there was nothing personal except my dressing table set and a Gaybox display shelf full of Wade Whimsies. My bedroom was strictly for sleeping. Bryn's was his den, studio, music room and library.

Tea was ready, and what a spread. After dainty sandwiches I was urged to sample all the cakes: iced fondant fancies, lemon meringue pie, coffee sponge sandwich and if I could fit it in, a slice of fruit cake or a chocolate cup cake. I couldn't, but I did manage a serving of trifle in a cut glass bowl with a silver dessert spoon. Phew! What a tea. So different from our high tea at home where we had substantial sandwiches with chunky cheese, and onion rings soaked in vinegar and pork pie and crisps and sausages on sticks. I was not used to a traditional afternoon tea complete with tea pot adorned by a knitted cosy.

My offer of help to clear the table was refused and Bryn and I returned to his room to sit on his bed and look at his sketch books. He reached under the bed and gave me a rather dusty pile of papers.

'I'll put some music on. Do you like jazz?' He queried.

'Very much. I've got about ten records,' I responded, going on to list my collection of Acker Bilk and Ian Menzies, Chris Barber and Kenny Ball.

'Lonnie Donegan too,' I continued. 'Although that's skiffle, not really jazz.'

'Er, yes…um, I mean real jazz.' He made a selection, took it deftly and reverently from the sleeve and placed the record tenderly on the turntable. The next twenty minutes were electrifying.

I looked at the art work, turning page after page of charcoal drawings, pen and ink sketches and water colours. Some, I could see were influenced by the great artists, Picasso, Mondrian, Matisse and even Gauguin. Most were original and I thought them very good, especially when compared to my own efforts.

My concentration was sometimes jarred by wild and soulful improvised music. I'd never heard jazz like it. When the record had finished I leant across to study the sleeve: John Coltrane.

'Like it?' Bryn asked. 'Jazz is my passion, especially pieces featuring the sax. I've got an old one somewhere under the bed, but I can't get a note out of it!'

A couple of hours passed quickly and it was soon time to walk to the bus stop.

'I'd like to lend you a few records if you'll have time to play them,' Bryn mused as I slipped my jacket on. 'Yes, I'll select three.' He knew exactly where to find them and quickly slipped the albums into a bag.

'Read the sleeve notes later. You'll miss the bus.'

When I got back to my room I drew the records out to look at the artists. Charles Mingus, Jimmy Yancey and Charlie 'Bird' Parker. These three were to form the basis of my life-long love of jazz and blues music and the names would soon become as familiar as my friends.

We met twice a week for the next three weeks and I soaked up more details of Bryn's life. He was a pacifist but had an academic interest in warfare, its whys and wherefores and the triggers for war. He studied battles and soldiers and belonged to the British Model Soldier Society. He spent hours crafting miniature figures, correct in every detail of their uniform. This needed meticulous research, so he visited regimental museums and pored over colour plates in library books. He would build up figures, uniforms and weapons from bits of old metal paint tubes, acrylic hardener and balsa wood. Tufts of bristle from a hearth brush would be a helmet plume, a cocktail stick made a lance.

I was introduced to his friends, Mike the artist, Kevin Ryland whose encyclopaedic knowledge of film and music in all its forms was incredible. There was John Spence and Ron Collier, who were jazz fans, and Trevor and Muriel Laidler who were artists and shared Bryn's deep love of Blues music. He had pen friends too, dotted round the world and he would write long intense letters about jazz or the Russian Revolution or Italian film directors or communism versus fascism.

My interest and involvement in all things artistic was at fever pitch. I knew I should be concentrating on my forthcoming exams. Two weeks before the first one was timetabled I told Bryn I could not see him until they were over. He said he would telephone from a call box or write. He would definitely keep in touch and we would see each other once exams were over.

As our relationship had blossomed so I had hoped that we would somehow stay in contact once college had finished. I had to make the final decision over which dairy I would work in and I finally selected the St. Ivel cheese factory at Westbury in Wiltshire. It was about half way between Redditch and Torquay and had excellent train connections. Perhaps I was hoping for too much but I felt we had grown too close to sever all links in a few weeks time.

I buckled down to revision and the examinations were suddenly in full flow. Results would follow in about two weeks and until then none of the students would know if they were eligible to take their National Diplomas. These were external exams held at the School of Agriculture at Reading University.

One step at a time I told myself, enjoy the last two or three weeks. There were outings and events and the Going Down Ball, but these weeks were dominated by my desire to see Bryn. We went to Plymouth and Exeter at weekends and looked round galleries and bookshops. We walked the wonderful parks of Torquay and along the coastal footpath. Some evenings we meandered round Newton Abbot and the surrounding lanes.

End of term was imminent and I could not bear to think that there was a chance that I might not see Bryn again. I asked my parents if I could bring a friend home to stay for a few days when I left college. Mum's voice was filled with apprehension and I assured her that she would like my new friend.

Having despatched my bulky luggage and trunk home via Carter Paterson I left Seale-Hayne College in June 1964 having completed my application to sit for my National Diploma in a couple of weeks time.

I looked out of the window as the train pulled out of Newton Abbot. Bryn sat bedside me looking rather conspicuous in his dated 1950s style suit with its pleated waist band and trouser turn-ups. He wanted to make a good first impression on my parents and had shaved his beard off and had a hair cut. I thought he looked nicer in his black tee shirt but I understood his reasoning. I felt confident that his quiet, polite manner and unassuming ways would make him an instant success with the family.

That's what I thought, but the reality did not match the expectation.

Chapter 15

∞ Make or break ∞

I t's the quiet ones you've got to watch,' Mum warned. 'They've got something to hide. Close. Secretive.'

'Oh, surely not,' I countered. 'Doesn't it mean that they just stand back and think about things? They don't just jump to conclusions immediately. The quiet ones, as you put it, want to properly think out an answer; to weigh up the facts.'

'No, not in my experience. They are usually devious. Thinking of ways to get back at you. Hatching plots.'

'Well Mum, he's not like that. He's quiet because he's overwhelmed. We're quite a boisterous fam…'

She interrupted,

'No, that's just it: family. He couldn't have the background. What does his father do? Did he go to grammar school? He just sat on the settee, not saying a word. You can't like him.'

I felt once again the need to justify myself, my friends, my choices. How could I, with a mother who seemed so biased and blinkered. She just did not understand me.

I tried.

'Well Mum, he's shy. He's sensitive. He's an artist.'

'What the hell do you mean, an artist? I thought he worked in a factory!'

I opened my mouth again, to explain.

'It's a printers' Mum, not just a factory. He's a craftsman; he's done a five-year apprenticeship. And yes, he is artistic. He's got a studio and writes poetry too.'

As soon as I had said it I realised it was red rag to a bull, and the bull charged.

'There you are then! He's not a proper man. You want someone to look after you, make decisions, not a quiet mouse like that.'

I was very close to tears. There was worse to come but I could not cope with it at the moment. I backed towards the kitchen door and pulled on the brass knob.

'He'll be different next time, Mum, now he's met you and Dad,' I said over my shoulder as I fled along the hall and made for the staircase and the cool sanctuary of my bedroom.

I lay on my bed and thought things through. I realised that things were not going very well and that my parents had not taken to my new boyfriend.

I had only just returned home after seeing Bryn off on the train, and already the inquiry had begun. I felt limp, drained by the interrogation from Mum. Bryn and I had spent six days together, doing the rounds. We had visited friends and relatives; and I had shown him local landmarks and the milestones of my life. Now, once again, I had hoped for approval, this time for my boyfriend. All I had got was dissatisfaction and negative vibes.

How could I tell my parents that on the very last evening of Bryn's visit, when we had returned home from the cinema and crept quietly upstairs to our rooms, Bryn had turned back on the top stair to say goodnight. It wasn't just 'goodnight.' He said,

'Will you consent to being my wife?'

I had rewound my life in two seconds, reliving its ups and downs and answered,

'Yes.'

We were unofficially engaged. We were so happy we wanted to shout it to the world. Instead of that, for the time being, it was a dark secret. We knew that Bryn would have to go through the ordeal of asking my father for his consent: I was not yet twenty-one.

The next week I was off to Reading with about fifteen other students from Seale-Hayne College to stay in university accommodation, while we sat for the National Diploma in Dairying. I did not feel quite so nervous now that the hurdle of the College Diploma was over.

I had a temporary summer job fixed up, working in the same office as Mum: the cost office at Terry's Spring Factory in Redditch. They were famous world-wide for bike saddles and angle-poise lamps, amongst other things. I was not sure if I would enjoy working at the next desk to Mum, but the figure work had to be accurate, and it kept my brain occupied. My emotions were elsewhere. Bryn and I wrote to each other every single day and I waited for the post to arrive before I set out with Mum for the office. Sometimes he would write a poem and once he used the back of a Lyons fruit pie packet, the only thing he had to hand when he felt like writing!

In our letters we had planned that I should visit Torquay for a weekend. I could stay in his sister's room while she was at a friend's house. Now, the visit was over, I was on my way home. What an exciting weekend it had been. I was clacking home on the train, oblivious, in my reverie, of the other passengers in the compartment.

My new ring seemed to glow through the suede of my brown leather shoulder bag. I just had to have another look. I laid my bag across my knees, zip towards me and pulled the metal tab across. I could see the cream box, imprinted on the top with 'The Gold Shop'. I put both my hands into the bag and eased the lid off revealing the engagement ring sitting neatly in the slot of its black velvet cushion.

I felt tingly from head to toe, and proud and guilty. The reason for my weekend visit to Torquay had been a secret. As far as my parents knew I was returning a visit to my boyfriend who had stayed a week in our family home in Redditch.

I glanced down again, focusing on the sparkle of my ring. How would I tell them? How could I word it? How even to approach the subject? Then, in the train carriage as we rattled into Bristol, and trying to look nonchalant, I prised the ring out of its box and using my bag as cover eased it onto the third finger of my left hand. It was beautiful and I was delighted with it. I had wanted a diamond and I wanted it simple and understated. Finally I had settled on a Victorian ring with a gypsy setting. A single stone set in a plain gold band. Bryn had been saving back money from his wage packet and had proudly handed over the cash as we exchanged embarrassed, loving glances with each other.

The ring was on my finger and I had withdrawn my hand from the bag and surreptitiously turned my knuckles towards the sunlight. The brilliant stone had reflected a spectrum of dazzling rays around the carriage like the mirrored ball at the Locarno ballroom. My heart was beating fast as I had casually folded my arms with my left hand resting on top. I had pretended to look out of the window at the approaching city but my eyes were riveted on the reflection of my wonderful ring. It was a token of our love and the seal on our promise to be married.

Our engagement day 17th August 1964.

Yet it was still a closely-guarded secret. I had been training for four years and finished my college course with two diplomas - at great expense and personal sacrifice from my parents. I had often been reminded that I was the only one in the family with 'brains' and it was my responsibility to use them. My own hard work and ambition were discounted. I was expected to make good, progress in my career, be single-minded. I had to repay them for their sacrifices. I was experiencing the most exciting time of my life and I could not talk about it.

As the train finally puffed into Birmingham, New Street, I slipped the ring off and tenderly replaced it in the protective box. I had two weeks to prime my parents before Bryn's next visit when he would have to formally approach my father for his permission to marry me. Until that hurdle was crossed the ring would have to stay hidden with my diary at the back of my dressing table drawer, under my headscarves. For those two weeks I would be conscious of it waiting to beam out its love-light to show the world our happiness.

We had sent and received fourteen more letters and now it was time for Bryn to visit again. The dreaded interview with Dad was happening, now. I kept looking out of the kitchen window to where Dad was sitting comfortably on the garden bench, in control. Bryn was squirming. He looked embarrassed and harassed. He shifted uncomfortably in the plastic chair, crossing and uncrossing his legs. Mum bustled in and out of the kitchen and feeling desperate I asked,

'Whatever do you think they're talking about?'

'Well, Daddy will want to know how much Bryn earns, how much he's got saved, where you are going to live when you are married, that sort of thing.'

'I know how much he earns, about £12 a week,' I supplied. 'And he's got a bit in the Post Office Savings Bank. About £20 I think.'

'That doesn't seem much for all those years of work,' Mum said accusingly. 'How old did you say he was?'

'It was his birthday last week. He was twenty-five,' I told her. 'Oh, when do you think they will finish talking?'

'I'll take a cup of tea down and see what I can find out,' Mum suggested, seeing that I was getting anxious.

As she walked down the garden with the tray Dad stood up and shook Bryn's hand. It was over, and through the open door I heard my father say,

'You have assured me that you love her and I trust you to make her happy. Good luck to both of you.'

I rushed down the path and gave Dad a hug and turned to Bryn who looked worn to a frazzle and very relieved that the last hour and a half was over.

'I'll get the ring,' I whispered, kissing him briefly, and flew up to my bedroom to unearth the box from my drawer. By the time I returned to the garden my parents had moved indoors and Bryn and I were left alone. He slipped the ring onto my finger telling me how much he loved me.

We wandered dreamily into the house just as Mum and Dad were pouring out a glass of sherry for each of us.

'Just as long as you're happy, ducky,' Dad said as he passed my glass.

Events in my life were moving fast and soon it would be time to travel to London along with the other new recruits to the United Dairies Central Laboratory where I would begin my specialised training for the work I would be performing at the cheese factory. I had only visited London on a couple of occasions. Once on a school trip, aged eleven, and then on a coach outing with Mum's office. I knew about the West End, the theatres, and Piccadilly Circus and that was about it. Accommodation had been arranged for us and feeling very provincial and conspicuous I made my way nervously from Euston station by tube to South Kensington.

Chapter 16

⌒ My own person? ⌒

I was on my own. Free at last. I could make what I wanted of my life now. I was responsible for my own decisions and my own mistakes. It was down to me to find my way round London and to the accommodation that had been booked for the new recruits. I fumbled self-consciously with my map whilst standing in a shop doorway. Hornton Street; there it was. Just got to cross over, and the road was almost opposite. Kensington Library would be a landmark.

I found my way to the street and wandered along the terraces looking for number twenty-nine. The residential hotel took up a long stretch of the street and I located the door to reception. They told me that United Dairies had made a block booking and my friends were on the same corridor. I was relieved to see some familiar faces and we sat on a bed and compared notes. We had to report to the Central Laboratory at White City at eight-thirty the next morning. We consulted our tube maps and worked out the routes and the changes. Breakfast the following morning was early to allow us to reach the lab by the set time.

The following six weeks were spent learning and perfecting the laboratory tests and techniques that were unique to the dairy we were destined for. The work was demanding, even compared to college chemistry and microbiology practical sessions. The products at the St. Ivel factory in Westbury, Wiltshire, that I was destined for, were all processed cheeses. I had not appreciated previously that this was a whole different ball game. The manufacturing process was completely different. Cheese, butter, milk powder and the like were the raw ingredients not the finished product as in most other dairies. I had inadvertently drawn the short straw as far as the work went. We all plodded on, rigidly adhering to the strict procedures laid down by head office and the central laboratory, slowly learning our skills; until six

Me, in love and ready for anything.

weeks later we were deemed trained, and were allowed to move to our chosen dairies and head the teams of laboratory technicians.

Social life in London was a different thing entirely. Sometimes we would go out in a group on a shopping or window shopping spree. Usually I felt content to wander round on my own, soaking up the atmosphere of London. I would browse along Kensington Church Street looking in bookshops and antique shops. I would drift along Kensington High Street admiring the fashions in the boutiques and stores and sometimes I would be a complete tourist and watch the Changing of the Guard or walk along the Embankment.

Bryn managed to visit on three occasions while I stayed in London. He knew the capital quite well and my horizons were broadened by visits to Art Cinemas and Jazz Clubs. We trawled the record shops such as Dobell's for elusive jazz albums and I spent hours in the huge HMV store, propped against the fittings while Bryn thumbed his way through endless records. Foyle's bookshop in Charing Cross Road was another Mecca for us and we would usually be tempted to buy a book each.

When Bryn came to visit, he usually crashed out in the bedroom of one of the girls who had gone home for the weekend. The idea of sleeping together before we were married was still taboo. Even when we had an opportunity, as in London, all we managed was a guilty ineffectual tussle. In other respects we were the image of a newly engaged couple; holding hands constantly, twining arms, gazing into each others eyes. It must have made my friends sick. There was also an unwritten restriction at work. When we had attended the selection interviews we had all been asked if we were engaged or shortly intended to be. I had answered, in all truth, no. However my diamond ring now blazed conspicuously on my finger and whenever possible I hid it from the scrutiny of our senior tutors at Central Laboratory. I guess they thought that a girl with her mind on marriage would not have her mind on work.

I made excuses not to visit home. I was having too good a time in London. In any case, I had only just escaped from parental restrictions. Here, I was free to decide how to spend my leisure time and my money. The starting salary for all of us Senior Laboratory Technicians or Bacteriologists was £600 a year and for the time being at least, I felt I deserved a few new clothes. I had always made my own dresses, blouses and coats, and knitted my own jumpers but here in London all my clothes looked a bit homespun. I carefully chose some co-ordinating items from M&S although I really wanted half of Carnaby Street.

Towards the end of October, feeling very sophisticated after my brief encounter with the bright lights and big city, I packed my bags and left for a weekend in Redditch before moving to Westbury. I took the train down to Wiltshire on the Sunday with a suitcase of clothes to see me through six weeks at the residential hotel booked and subsidised by United Dairies.

The Cedar Hotel was a pleasant, old fashioned establishment set back from the Warminster Road with the eponymous conifer with its evergreen fingers pointing artistically at the back of the range of buildings. It was furnished largely in Edwardian style, and I wondered if the side tables, standard lamps and battered armchairs were the last relics from the homes of the aged and genteel residents. The oak staircase, with its gothic-style carved newel posts, led round a dogleg bend to the spotless bedrooms which, despite crisply laundered bed-linen, had a slightly musty smell. The bathroom was on the half-landing and the aged geyser loomed over the bath which showed grey smudges of cast iron through the worn enamel.

After dinner I wandered with three elderly ladies across the hall where a fire burnt in the cast-iron grate. The oak fire-surround with more fancy carving and blue glazed tiles made me guess that the décor dated from the late nineteenth century, especially when I looked up to see a moulded plaster frieze on the ceiling. In the residents' lounge a gas fire plopped cosily from the tiled hearth and a maid came in to draw the curtains. I was soon aware that everyone had their special place and as a newcomer I was furthest from the fire, but at least I had a high backed winged armchair to shield me from the draughty doorway. The old ladies arranged their glasses on the end of their noses and fumbled in bags for their crochet work, knitting or embroidery. Having tried all these crafts I was able to take an interest and ask questions and so my probationary evening passed until at about nine o'clock they toddled off to bed. This was to form the pattern of most of my evenings at The Cedar except on the occasions when Bryn would come up on the train from Torquay for the weekend. Not anxious to return to his very basic guest house he would escort me to the cinema further down the main road. It had a tin roof and sometimes, if it was raining, the dialogue was drowned out by the sound of the rain pelting on the roof.

It was not easy to fit in at the Cheese Factory, as it was known to the locals. The factory was at the far end of the town, very near the station, on an area known as the Ham. The low dairy buildings were fronted by a brick built office block in a vague 1930s style with a moderately impressive entrance. Scattered round the yard were other storage buildings which housed the raw materials, the packing materials and the finished products waiting for despatch. I was shown round by the production manager after a welcoming handshake from the boss, Mr Driscoll.

I was introduced to the laboratory staff who were all working feverishly. The matriarch was Mrs Haine who had been there since the year dot. She was a helpful and kindly woman who, over the months, tried to make my job easier. Trouble was, to some extent I was taking over the work that she had done for decades. She was in charge of the quality control of all the products and did extensive keeping-quality tests on everything, cutting open the packaging, smelling the products for deterioration and storing them at different temperatures for different lengths of time, to see how they would keep. My brief was to develop bacteriological and chemical tests that would run alongside these elementary but important physical checks. I would need all the tact and diplomacy I could muster not to alienate Mrs. Haine and swoop in as a new girl, fresh from college, and radically alter all the procedures that had been in place for years.

The other staff were pleasant young women who had come to the lab straight from school and were responsible for the statutory chemical tests on the products, things like fat content and moisture percentage. They worked in a rota devised by Mrs Haine and collected samples from the factory production area, from the raw ingredients and from the finished packs of processed cheese. One of them was responsible for preparing the laboratory and clearing up.

In my first few weeks I had to get a grip on staff politics as well as learn all the production methods and develop a detailed insight into all the lab procedures that were in place. I could sense a slight resentment and sometimes caught the tail-end of whispered conversations. In some cases they were right: they did know more about it than I. I felt they ganged up on me, withheld essential information, made my life difficult. I had been academically trained and had adequate practical experience but no one thought it necessary to include any supervisory skills in our college course. I floundered in my efforts between trying to command respect and the need to work alongside these staff and learn the nitty-gritty of the system. I desperately needed a friend. Instead of that I had to tick them off for being late for work, spending too much time on tea breaks or staying in the loo for a fag.

My immediate tasks were to section off one part of the lab for bacteriological tests, develop these tests with some advice from Central Laboratory in London and to order all the equipment including glassware, incubators and all the different growing media for a range of bacteria. I selected one of the existing staff to be my assistant and organised a programme of basic training in microbiology for her.

I felt very ambivalent about going to work. On one hand I felt excited by the scope and complexity of my work, and of the need to put all my skills to use but on the other hand I felt out of my depth with the staffing issues and my complete lack of experience as a supervisor and the difficulty of delegating work that I was not completely familiar with myself. The first six weeks were something of a probationary period and as they passed so I became more confident in my own work and my handling of the existing staff.

My accommodation at The Cedar Hotel, Westbury, had been subsidised by my company for six weeks and I had been looking for new lodgings in the town. I finally took a room in a pretty little terraced cottage in Edward Street not far from The Marketplace. My elderly landlady was Mrs Coult and she was a gentlewoman of the old type. On the day my parents arrived to assist me with moving in she agreed with them the need to look after me in all respects. I heard her say that she would never allow my visiting fiancé to set one foot on the staircase!

Whilst I had resided at The Cedar Hotel Bryn had come up from Torquay to see me several times and stayed in a B&B. He had decided to leave his job at the Teignmouth Press and look for work at a printer's in Wiltshire. He had attended an interview at Dotesios, book and jobbing printers at Bradford on Avon about seven miles from Westbury. He also needed to look for digs in the area and spent one of his weekend visits scouring the postcards in shop windows looking for accommodation adverts.

Just before I moved into 12, Edward Street, Bryn moved into Old Alfred House. Essentially it was a flop-house for the itinerant Irish navvies working on the new cement works at Westbury. The ancient, L-shaped, half-timbered building, formerly a medieval hall-house, had been divided up with stud-partitioning to give lots of small cubicle-like bedrooms. They were just big enough to squeeze in a bed, a bedside locker and a chest of drawers. A hook on the back of the door provided hanging space. The walls were so thin that Bryn said he could hear every intimate noise from the rooms each side. The bathroom facilities were very basic and the toilets were a sight to behold. The encrusted wooden seats were permanently hooked up onto the water pipe that led down from the high level cistern. As a gesture to hygiene the newspaper carefully arranged over the floor was changed daily. The low-ceilinged dining room housed many tables complete with plastic cloths, sugar bowls, sauce bottles and ashtrays.

We could be together as often as work permitted now. We lived only about a three minute walk from each other. I had hoped that we could meet up in the mornings and walk together the mile and a half down to the Ham. Unfortunately Bryn's train to Bradford on Avon left earlier than my starting time at the cheese factory so we had to wait until the evening to meet. We explored the lanes and villages of the surrounding area, walking for miles, happily swinging our clasped hands between us. We would venture by train into Bath, spending days in record and book shops. Often in the evenings we would go to one of the many cinemas in the city. Sometimes we would visit the tiny, tinny cinema in Westbury. We were ecstatically happy. We were completely wrapped up in each other, wanting little other company. It never occurred to me that no sooner had I achieved a sort of independence and the chance to become my own person than I gave myself to someone else. I was part of a couple, a unit, not independent after all.

On as many weekends as we could, we would try to get away from Westbury and our lodgings and visit friends or family. I loved going down to Torquay. The visits always had a holiday atmosphere about them. The last section of the wonderful train journey was along the bank of the River Exe and then the line turned south along the coast to Dawlish to where the track skirted the beach and waves sometimes surged up over the train. After Teignmouth we had the pleasure of the Teign estuary before the train reached Newton Abbot and began the inland section to Torquay. Once we had made our way with our luggage across town to Upton we dragged slowly up the stony track to Stantaway House. There was always a smiling welcome from Bryn's Mum. She was, and still is, a wonderfully positive woman, always seeing the best in people and situations. She would tell us anecdotes of minor personal disasters that would have many people completely fazed but she seemed always to see the funny side.

Bryn and I would spend our visit imbibing the ozone along the coastal footpaths or walking across sandy beaches. We would visit the scattering of relatives and thank them for our engagement presents. In the evenings we might go to one of the three cinemas in Torquay or more often visit Bryn's friends.

Mike Tolliday had a flat in another area of Torquay. We would sit round clutching our mugs of black coffee having intense discussions about the meaning of art, existentialism, poetry, politics, painting techniques or the effect of light on landscape. This kind of socialising was still quite new to me, despite two years at college. It represented a freedom, not just of ideas and a way of expressing them, but of the opportunity to express them. I began to realise that not everyone filled their time with either working or doing chores. This had been slowly dawning on me since I had met Bryn. At first it seemed completely alien to my strong work ethic and the feeling that you defined yourself by what you did, by your achievements. Now I was beginning to accept that leisure and culture had a part to play. The hours would pass, a candle in a straw-covered Chianti bottle might be lit, the curtains were rarely drawn. We would shift around in our battered chairs or put a velvet cushion on the floor to sprawl on. We rarely had any alcohol to drink; in fact Bryn hardly ever had even a half a pint of beer. We were on a buzz but it was not chemically produced, it was the sheer excitement of ideas, new concepts and wonderful things to see and experience.

Some weekends it would be Muriel and Trevor that we visited. They were artists and I loved their bohemian lifestyle. They had eloped to get married and had a young son. Their home featured their paintings and designs and there was colour and texture everywhere. Like Bryn they were passionate jazz fans and also like Bryn they adored The Blues. They had a piano and Muriel would sing songs that had been recorded by Mama Yancey, Bessie Smith and Billie Holliday. Her blonde hair would fall forward over her face as she played, and then she would toss it back revealing her heavily made-up, beautiful eyes.

I envied her confidence and talent but most of all I envied her looks. I felt very plain beside her. I still had my hair very short with just a sort of little pom-pom fringe but at last I had thinned down with quite a skinny waist and shapely legs. I applied my eye make-up in the Elizabeth Taylor-Cleopatra style of the time but I never felt glamorous. I never developed that air of mystery and uncertainty that some women seem to have. But what did it matter? Bryn loved me and wanted to marry me.

On the odd Saturday afternoon when we were down in Torquay we used to call on Kevin Ryland who lived with his parents in a charming Regency-style house in Abbey Road. We would be ushered into the rather badly lit hall which was hung with the most beautiful pre-Raphaelite paintings and then we passed into Kevin's inner sanctum where he kept his enormous record collection and hi-fi equipment. We would sit on an uncomfortable, ancient settle, slightly softened by battered silk or tapestry cushions and spend hours listening to the most wonderful music. Kevin impressed me with his encyclopaedic knowledge of music and the lists of catalogue numbers stored in his memory. While the music played there would often be a reverent hush until the stylus was lifted with care and precision from the pristine vinyl.

Talk would be of music and art, the shows running at different galleries, and of avant-garde art films. I loved it, and soaked up the atmosphere. After a while Kevin's mother might appear from the hall and ask what we would like to eat or drink. Ages later she would appear in another doorway from a different direction bearing a lacquer tray of biscuits and tea. I was baffled by this unexpected manifestation until I realised that the house had two staircases.

Mrs Ryland was a fascinating woman with an unconventional appearance that I loved. Her fine hair would be screwed back into a wispy bun revealing her attractive bone structure and strangely compelling eyes. She dressed in many layers, usually topping every thing with a baggy cardigan or even an old jacket. I felt she had many tales to tell and would have loved to spend more time with her and listen to her recollections. Sometimes we would be invited into the front sitting room where Mr Ryland would be surrounded by newspapers and pages of The Times Literary Supplement, with his chair drawn as close as possible to the paraffin stove. I always valued the time that Bryn and I spent with this family in their faded home which breathed beauty and culture.

Late on Sunday afternoon we would say goodbye to Bryn's parents and take the train back to reality and work. I was feeling increasingly discontent with both my living accommodation and my employment. I needed to address both issues, and soon.

Chapter 17

∽ A light at the end of the tunnel ∽

Christmas 1964 meant a visit to my parents' in Redditch and during that visit Bryn and I discussed our possible wedding date with Mum and Dad. Finally, September 1965 was decided upon.

We returned to Westbury feeling happy and I knew I had to resolve the areas of my life that were giving me anxiety. My accommodation situation had been far from satisfactory. My landlady watched me like a hawk and checked my every coming and going. As I returned home in the evenings after visiting Bryn I would leave Alfred Street and cross the square in front of the town hall and then I would see her bedroom curtains twitch as she heard my steps ringing out down the length of Maristow Street. I did not like it: I behaved properly and gave her no cause for concern, always paid my rent promptly and was polite.

I found other lodgings and in January moved to Prospect Square with Mr and Mrs Gummer. It was further to walk to work but the atmosphere in the house was much nicer and the Gummers respected my privacy. The square was well named for it was elevated and had a magnificent view across many miles of countryside. The houses in clusters of twos, fours and fives ranged round three sides of an open space where there were allotments. They had been built in an Arts and Crafts style in 1886 by W. H. Lufton in memory of his uncle. Bryn followed my lead and moved from the rather unsavoury Old Alfred House to a house across the square from me, at number twenty five.

The next things to sort out were the problems at work. I was feeling very put on. I felt I was being asked to do things that were not part of my brief. I had already extended my responsibilities to cover quality control of all packing materials including foil, polythene and cardboard. I tested the water supply, the machinery and the equipment. This was in addition to chemical and microbiological tests on ingredients and finished products. Now, it seemed I had to learn in detail about manufacturing processes of every product and make decisions about recipes and textures of the processed cheese in its various stages.

In the first instance I put my dissatisfaction to the person immediately above me in the hierarchy. This was the assistant manager, who said rather noncommittally that he would see what he could do. The months went by and nothing changed. I told him again that my work load was too great. I had to run from place to place in the factory to keep up with my schedule and I had begun to develop varicose veins: walking the mile and a half back to my digs in the evenings produced stabbing pains in my legs. My boss said he had mentioned my problems to the Manager who would look into it when he had the time.

This was not the only thing I did not like. There was a very strict observance of rank within the work force of the factory. Every one with a title, that is, above the description of foreman or forewoman, was 'staff' and everyone on the factory floor was 'workforce'. There was a separation even at meal times. Staff ate their meals in the Managers' dining room and had special cutlery and china, jugs of water on the table and silver-plated condiments; the workers had their meals in the canteen. I hated this. It was in direct opposition to my belief of equality and socialism. In addition I often had a solitary meal as the other half a dozen or so of our elite bunch had a different shift pattern to me.

I needed a friend and finally I found one. Wandering round the yards of the factory one lunch break I saw a cat disappear into the boiler house and I looked into the door to call it. I got into conversation with the boiler man and felt an immediate bond of comfort and relaxation. It reminded me of my days on the farm when the warmth of the boiler-house was a sanctuary from the miseries of the cold and a place to dry out my rain sodden clothes. After a few days visiting this retreat and enjoying the debates we had, I decided to bring sandwiches to work for my lunch and spend my break with George and the cat. I never knew if anyone was aware of my disregard for my position but no one ever mentioned it to me.

May of that year brought my twenty-first birthday and we had a small celebration at home. My parents bought me a Jones sewing machine and most of the other family members decided to give me something for our future home. Sylvia gave me a Saint Christopher medallion and her mum provided a beautiful big-linked silver chain.

Becoming twenty-one really was quite a big milestone. If I had still been living at home I would have been given the front door key to the house. Until then, as a 'minor' one was not considered responsible enough to come and go as one pleased. I would have to be home when my parents said and they would always be there waiting for my arrival, to check the time and see that I was safely in. As I lived away from home now, this was not quite so significant but I received several token keys in silver plastic with the fob shaped like 21.

My present from Bryn meant delayed gratification. I had already started to plan my honeymoon outfit and I realised it would be a struggle to buy everything that I wanted. Bryn had offered to buy the coat that I would wear when we set out from the wedding reception for the honeymoon that we planned in Paris. Naturally I wanted this coat to look really stylish and exude quality. We went up to Birmingham to choose something in the sales. I finally selected a cream, wool bouclé, wrap-around style with a gorgeously soft Lynx collar. I felt a million dollars in it. The fit and length were perfect and the fur collar enhanced my complexion. The only disappointment was that I could not wear it yet as I wanted it to be brand new for going away in on honeymoon. I had to wrap it in its polythene bag and hang it in the back of the wardrobe for four months.

I was very excited by the thought of our forthcoming marriage. I did not have a second thought. I was desperately in love and could not wait for the time when we would be officially united in front of the whole family and all our friends. I felt completely confident that I would cope with all the practical responsibilities of looking after a home, in fact, with the arrogance of youth I thought I would do it better than anyone had ever done it! I looked forward to the sharing of things like shopping and cleaning, of us both working to put our joint income into our home and everything we would need. I dreamt what it would be like to be together all the time, to share every minute of leisure with the man I loved. There were practical details to be attended to, as well.

I had to decide on a design for my wedding dress and find a dressmaker to put my dream into reality, I had to complete my honeymoon outfit and I had to liaise with my parents to finalise the plans for the wedding and reception. Most importantly, we had to find somewhere to live.

Word of our imminent marriage had got back to Bryn's employers and one day the manager asked to see him. He told Bryn that the company owned some properties nearby but they had not been occupied for some while. They had been acquired to house families of employees moving in to the district at a time when the workforce was much more mobile and people changed their jobs almost on a whim. He asked if we would like to look at a flat that was actually within the complex of factory buildings. In fact it was on the top floor of the building that housed the Linotype machines at the printing factory.

After work one evening I crossed the road from the cheese factory and walked down over the bridge to the railway station. I passed under the chestnut trees and down the ramp that cut off the corner and walked up the approach road to the low station building with its twin gables. As I waited for the train to steam up the track I wondered what sort of place Bryn's manager was going to show us. I had been to the printing factory at Bradford on Avon to meet Bryn from work and could not imagine that there was anywhere that could provide accommodation. As the train set me down at my destination I looked down the track and through the length of the tunnel to where I would walk over the level crossing. I had to take the long way round of course but soon I was turning down Bridge Street beside the twelfth-century bridge. Passing ancient buildings in mellow stone and then overhanging hedgerows I finally reached the level crossing. I could see the crossing keeper in his hut having a brief sit down having re-opened the gate for traffic after my train had passed through, five minutes earlier.

I could hear the sound of the weir now as I approached the mill building. Greenland Mills had been built in the nineteenth century as a cloth mill serving the sheep-rich county of Wiltshire. Now, the rambling cluster of buildings that extended on up the lane housed a printer's, a rubber factory and a sports car manufacturer.

Bryn was waiting on the forecourt of the factory with the manager who was jangling a bunch of keys.

'The flat is on the top floor of that building there,' he nodded towards a substantial four-square building, solidly constructed of Bath stone. It used to be the mill-manager's house but for many years now has been our office block. Dotesios has been here since 1905.'

As we walked across the road I somehow expected him to go into the impressive front door but instead he made his way to the right hand side of the building, explaining as we followed him,

'Your fiancé will already know this but the first floor houses our linotype department and the machines can be quite noisy at times. Still, the men have usually clocked off by the time you will get back from work.'

Bryn had already explained to me that the long rows of type were cast from molten metal in this department. Someone tapped the text into a machine and slugs of words, all back to front, came out ready to be set onto forms and screwed into the quoins of the printing machine. It was a noisy, dirty job and Bryn was glad that he was a machine minder with the responsibility of actually operating the huge letterpress machine that printed the words onto the paper.

We turned the corner of the building and moved along the side where an outcrop of ferns betrayed a leaking gutter. Rounding the back of this once grand building we faced a flight of steep steps which, part way up were covered by a canopy. It was damp, dark and dismal. Overhanging trees dripped beads of moisture, feeding lichens and ferns on the mossy bank. Rocky outcrops loomed out from the undergrowth and I gave an involuntary shiver despite the June sun still shining round the front.

The boss led the way leaving Bryn and I trailing behind exchanging doubtful glances. He turned the key in the lock and we could smell the damp billowing out of the door. Another flight of stairs took us up to a landing with a door at each end. One was labelled 1a and the other 1b. We looked at each flat and noticed that the one on the western end of the building would get more sun. Could we really live here in this musty flat that had not been occupied for over ten years? We pricked up our ears when the manager began talking about the rent.

'We have kept these flats especially for our employees and continuing to work for us would be a condition of the tenancy. However, we do not charge a huge rent and I could offer you either flat for twenty five shillings a week, (one pound, twenty five pence). You would have a free range over how you decorate it and we would not mind if you put up shelves or added kitchen cupboards.'

By now Bryn and I wanted time on our own to discuss the possibility of living at Greenland Mills. We walked up the lane towards the level crossing, soaking up the romantic atmosphere of this old tree-lined lane. The river bank was in dappled shade where the willows and alders hung over the water and the incessant rush of the water pouring over the weir reminded us of the

My lodgings, Prospect Square, Westbury.

rusty axle of the mill wheel protruding from one of the buildings. There were no street lights and we would have no neighbours. I could picture Bryn walking up towards town to meet me in the evenings when I stepped from the train. He knew he must never be tempted to take a short cut up the tunnel beside the crossing gates. The station could be easily seen and he would hear my train departing from the platform once I had alighted, then it would rush through the tunnel and clatter over the crossing.

We talked about what we could do to the flat to make it into our first home and marvelled at the cheapness of the rent. It would certainly be convenient for Bryn; he would only have to cross the road to go to work, and it would not be too difficult for me. The cheese factory was close to the station at Westbury. In winter I could wait for the train either end of my journey in a cosy waiting room warmed by a blazing coal fire. We were desperate to get out of lodgings and as a newly married couple would enjoy the privacy of this remote location. As we sat on the train returning to Westbury and our digs we planned how we would be able to exist on Bryn's pay and save most of mine towards the deposit of the house we wanted to buy in the future.

The next day Bryn knocked on the manager's door.

'We'd like to take the flat. We'll be getting married in September and wondered if we could start work decorating the flat in our spare time.'

The boss moved from his desk to a cupboard and took out two keys tied together with a piece of string. He passed them over to Bryn, saying,

'You may as well have them straight away. You will need all the time you can get to do the place up in three months. We won't charge you any rent until you move in.'

The next weekend we went to Redditch to tell my parents the good news. They seemed pleased but reserved judgement until they had viewed our future home. In fact I still had the feeling that Mum and Dad were not overjoyed with my choice of husband-to-be. They were not exuding happy vibes on our behalf and never extended Bryn the open-armed welcome I thought he deserved.

Dad lent us his Mini and we took the opportunity to visit friends and relatives as well as discuss the details of our forthcoming wedding. Granny and Grandad Winnett were delighted to see us but I noticed that Grandad seemed rather vague and guessed that senility was setting in. He had wandered off, up the back fields, once or twice lately and Gran was beside herself with worry.

Auntie Chris had been working for some time at Bunting's grocery shop in Alcester. It was a delightful shop near the church gates and at the start of Butter Street. Auntie worked in the office doing the wages and accounts and we were allowed to wend our way through the ancient half timbered shop and up the twisted stairs to the office where Auntie worked. She was excited to hear that we had found a place to live and promised to make us something nice for our flat.

I could not see Auntie Daye as she and Uncle Joe were visiting their cottage in Stratford upon Avon that weekend.

When we met Sylvia she wanted to know if I had decided on the pattern for her bridesmaid dress. Despite bursting into tears on the evening I had told her I was going to get married she had agreed to be my chief bridesmaid and look after the two little ones, my nieces Sue and Louise Reeves. I knew that as soon as we returned to Westbury I must finalise the patterns and fabrics. Since leaving the sixth form at school Sylv had worked in a bank and done a business studies course, but now she was getting itchy feet and wanted to train for something a bit more fulfilling.

Judy Davies was engaged and her wedding was planned for New Years' Day 1966. Her fiancé was a colleague in the Inland Revenue office where she worked.

Jane Adams was going to marry her farmer boyfriend and her future was mapped out for her. Any news I had of old school friends confirmed my feelings that I was rather unconventional. I had moved away from home as soon as possible, I was going to marry a man from a different part of the county and my interests all bordered on the bohemian. Yes, I was different, and I enjoyed it.

Mum and Dad definitely did not. They still longed for me to confirm, to behave in a ladylike way, to have long hair and wear high heeled shoes. I could sense their disapproval in their voices and body language. Well, I thought, this is me and that's it! Bryn had helped me to reinvent my artistic side and I felt complete: completely happy, completely sure and completely content.

After Sunday lunch Mum and Dad said they needed to discuss our wedding reception and invitations. They had decided that they could afford sixty guests. Things were a little better now, financially. Dad was still working, and he would not retire when he was sixty, a few days after my wedding. Mum was in the cost office at Terry's spring factory and had had a wage rise. Steve was in the Royal Airforce, stationed at Credenhill, near Hereford and training to be a chef, so he was self sufficient. My parents, for the first time in their lives, felt comparatively affluent.

They had investigated a few possibilities for the location of the reception and told us that the most likely was the Montfort Hotel at the top of Parsons Road, a little way up Mount Pleasant. We could drive up and have a look if we liked. They had asked a local printer for a book showing samples of wedding invitations and next time we visited Redditch we would be able to choose the design. Mum had started to draw up a list of people to invite. When I took the list from her hands I was horrified.

'But Mum, I had no idea we had so many relatives. Surely there must be at least twenty there without anybody's children. Then I see you've added all the neighbours and your friends.'

'They are people we've known for years. They have always taken such an interest in you, of course we must invite them,' Mum pronounced. 'You will be able to invite about fifteen of your friends, surely that's O.K?'

'I suppose so,' I sighed. 'I'll start to put a few names together when we get back home.'

'This is your home,' Mum snapped. 'And will always be.'

That evening, on the train going back to Westbury, I reckoned up how many places I had lived in since I was born. I had had seventeen addresses and had been bumped along from pillar to post. Now finally, I could look forward to a home of my own.

Chapter 18

∽ Ticking all the boxes ∽

I could hardly believe that it was under three months until Bryn and I got married. There was so much still to do. I had to cope with the increasing stress of going to work as well as help to decorate our flat, choose new clothes, get my wedding dress made, make compromises with my parents and visit Bryn's Mum and Dad in Torquay. I made a list to tick off, as I worked my way through the preparations.

I scoured the pattern books for a wedding dress that I liked. I knew what I did not want: nothing fussy, flounced or full. I wondered if a plain wedding dress existed. Finally I found almost the perfect pattern. The long dress was simple and gently shaped; it had a scooped neck and long narrow sleeves that ended in a slightly gathered cuff. I could not resist looking immediately for the material that would bring the picture to life. I needed two fabrics, one as the under-layer and another net or lace to go over the top. I walked back and forth along the racking in Rackhams and then made my choice. I would have pure white, heavily patterned, soft French lace over the whitest, figured, heavy brocade. I called the shop assistant to the huge rolls of material to confirm that the fabrics would work well together. Pleased with my choice I returned to Redditch to display my purchases. Mum had been disappointed that I wanted to go alone to Birmingham, but I knew that something as important as my wedding dress must be my decision and mine alone.

I took the material back to Westbury and made an appointment with the dressmaker that I had been recommended. A measuring session was arranged and soon I was going for my first fitting. Once the dress had been cut out I sent the pattern to Sylvia, my chief bridesmaid. I wanted her dress to mirror mine, but with only the brocade fabric.

I had pictured the effect I wanted to create. I would be in dazzling white with Bryn in his black suit. I wanted a simple bouquet of white flowers with long, trailing, dark green ivy leaves. Mum said lilies would look beautiful and I readily agreed this pre-Raphaelite look. Sylvia's dress would be ivy-green and her flowers would be white rosebuds, while the two little girls would wear soft gold-coloured satin dresses. Right, sorted: I could tick that box.

I thought I had better go with Bryn when he bought his suit and we went to Burtons in Torquay. It was so unusual to see Bryn dressed in anything formal, it was a surprise to register just how handsome he was. Although he was not quite six feet tall, his broad shoulders, slim hips and slight build gave an illusion of height and the narrow lapels tapering to the three low buttons of the long jacket looked expensive and distinguished. We felt that his £17 had been well spent. Another tick.

We needed a change from clothes shopping and decided to invest some time and energy into decorating our new flat. Bryn was as excited as I and we planned the colour schemes stage by stage. The kitchen would be blue and white. It faced the high bank at the back of the building so it needed light walls and the blue would have to come from accessories and the blue check curtains I had made. We chose two new base units and two glass fronted wall cupboards from the Liden whitewood range and went on the train to Haskins at Shepton Mallet to order them. While we were at the store we could not resist two kitchen stools with plain beech legs and blue and white vinyl tops. Dad had told us he would make a fold-down table to fix onto the wall as space was limited in the kitchen and the stools could be brought out of the corner to use with our table flap. Bryn's parents had promised us a cooker for our wedding present and one weekend we walked to the gas showroom to choose it. My parents offered to buy us a twin-tub washing machine and they said they would deliver it for us.

The rather damp smelling bathroom faced the dank, dripping trees as well. Magnolia coloured walls would warm it up and any colour bath mats would go with that. The three other rooms would be more of an interior design challenge and we were keen to put into use our ideas about colour combinations and style.

We had always liked the living room since the very first day we had viewed the flat. It was the two windows that made the difference. The room was light and bright and you could look out, along the road towards the level crossing, and see who was coming or on the other side you looked over the top of the printing factory to the trees that skirted the river bank. We thought the room could take some strong, bold colours and went to look through some wallpaper books in Bath where we thought the choice would be more adventurous. We had seen a contemporary three piece lounge suite that we liked in Knees's furniture shop in Trowbridge and wondered if we could form a colour scheme round the fabric.

Standing in the decorating shop we pictured the furniture. It was Scandinavian in style and had a sleek wooden frame in varnished teak. The seat and back cushions were upholstered in an attractively textured, brown tweed fabric, liberally flecked in red, orange and yellow. We nodded to each other in agreement; there were plenty of colours there to co-ordinate our walls and accessories. With new energy we turned the pages of wallpaper samples. Suddenly out of the page pounced a startling in-your-face flame red. It was a new paper, textured like wood chip but strongly coloured in a dense matt pigment. We turned the page to see a bright acid yellow paper in the same series. We knew immediately that these were the wallpapers we wanted. The vermillion paper would go on two opposite walls and the yellow on the other two. Yes, we would have to double-check the suite covers to confirm that both the red and yellow were the same as those before us but we both carried colours well in our mind's eye and felt very confident that we had the basis of a modern colour scheme.

Next weekend we ordered the furniture and the wallpaper and began thinking about the other things we would need. My savings had been steadily growing once our wedding day had been fixed and if we used Bryn's pay for train fares, cinema tickets and the odd cup of tea my salary could mount up to buy items for our home. We chose a teak standard lamp and I decided to have a go at making a huge shade. A long, low coffee table would be essential. Friends decided to club together to buy us one for a wedding present. Another present for this room was offered by Auntie Chris. She said she would choose some co-ordinating fabric and make us cushion covers and shades for a table lamp and pendant light. In due course these were delivered and featured apples, oranges and pears in all their vibrant ripe colours on a brown background. We wanted bookcases to complete the furniture in the living room, but we could not bring Bryn's up from Torquay on the train and mine from home would not be big enough for all the books. We would have to look for one. We also needed to find a suitable floor covering for the worn and pitted floorboards. Luck was with us because in a clearance sale we found a much reduced, pure wool, Wilton carpet piece just about the right size, and in a perfect, dark, chocolate brown which would be an excellent foil for the singing walls. It was delivered to the flat and we cut it to shape using a craft knife.

We chose a huge, plain, square-cornered wardrobe, big enough for us to share and felt very sophisticated when the salesman said it was in sapele wood, albeit, veneered.

We were running short of money by now and knew the double bed would be the last thing we could afford. Perhaps we could scrounge a chest of drawers from someone. We did even better than that. My parents came to visit us one day and we showed them the more picturesque parts of Westbury where I was still lodging. As we walked down Maristow Street from the Marketplace we saw some furniture outside a second hand shop. Amongst the assorted items was a large painted chest of drawers with an enormous capacity. It was priced two pounds but it was two pounds we did not have.

'Leave it to me, ducky,' Dad said, 'I'll see what I can do.'

Minutes later Dad came out rubbing his hands.

'Thirty bob (one pound fifty pence),' he smiled. 'That alright?'

We carted it over to Bradford on Avon sticking out of the back of the Mini, and lumped it up the steps to the flat. That would have to be it, for the bedroom. We would have a bed, a wardrobe and a chest; other bits of furniture could wait. The dining room would have to wait too. We could drape a cloth over the old paint-covered pasting table if we had guests and bring in the kitchen stools, the old bathroom chair and a wooden tea-chest as seats.

Dad and Mum had brought down the box of wedding invitations that had recently arrived from the printers. Bryn cast a professional eye over the quality of printing and silver embossing.

'Not bad,' he said. 'I couldn't have done much better myself.'

'Did you bring the list of guests?' I asked Mum. 'We could get on with writing them out. They could be sent at the end of the week if we get a move on.'

Mum fished the list out of her handbag and I scanned it. There were over thirty relatives and more than a dozen family friends. A mere twelve places were available for our friends, but I knew the money for our wedding had been hard saved, so I did not mention it.

I looked over Bryn's shoulder to admire the invitations once again, and noticed the unconventional wording. I thought better of commenting now but that evening when we were on our own, I said to Bryn,

'Did you see what it said on the first line of the invitations? Instead of saying 'Mr & Mrs J. Claysmith request the pleasure…' it says 'James and Mary Claysmith…' Don't you think that's odd?'

'I wonder if it's something to do with your funny family set up,' Bryn mused. 'Don't forget Jean told you that they could not be married until your father was divorced.'

I suddenly realised that this confirmed what I had always suspected: my parents were still not able to be married and could not, in all honesty, call themselves 'Mr & Mrs'.

Each evening that week we wrote out a few invitations and addressed the envelopes. By Friday we were ready to put them in the box outside the Post Office in The Shambles, at Bradford.

There were very few things left to do before our wedding in September. Headless Cross Methodist church was booked for the wedding service and Graham Moseley would play the organ. My dress was almost ready and the bridesmaid's dresses were finished. Mum was looking after the flowers, both the bouquets and the buttonholes. Trevor Laidler was to be Bryn's best man and he and Muriel would stay the night at our neighbours'. The Montville Hotel was booked and the buffet was organised for the reception. I had ticked each item off on my list. Only a few things remained to be done. I needed some more clothes and some accessories to wear with my lovely lynx-collared coat and we needed to finalise the plans for our honeymoon.

We knew that we were becoming totally obsessed by our wedding plans but the truth was, the big day was only a few weeks away. We decided to go into Bath for a day out. We loved the approach by train. Through Trowbridge first, then Bradford on Avon and across the level crossing that we now knew so well. The next part of the journey was not quite so familiar. We followed both the River Avon and the Kennet and Avon canal for long portions of the journey, passing through Avoncliff, Freshford and Limpley Stoke and the famous Dundas Aqueduct. Finally the train line snaked into Bath from the east giving us a wonderful view of Georgian terraces and crescents.

Bryn and I had been to this beautiful city a few times during the last year and enjoyed visiting the museum and art gallery and then wandering through the indoor market. This particular Saturday we had just finished browsing through the racks of books and passed along to Cavill's second hand furniture stall. Suddenly we spotted, on top of a pile of carefully balanced furniture, an old rocking chair. It had a high back crafted out of finely turned spindles and a jutting out head-rest each side topped off with delicately turned finials. All the wood including the shapely carved rockers was covered with a sticky black paint but the rush seat was in very good condition.

'Could you get that chair down, for us to look at please?' we called to the stallholder.

He penetrated the tangled mass of furniture and grasped a rocker then deftly swung it to the ground. He moved away for a few minutes giving us chance to look at it.

'I love it,' I said to Bryn. 'I don't think I've ever seen a chair like it. It's quite different from Dad's rocker.'

'How much do you want for it?' Bryn called across the concrete gangway.

'Twenty five bob (one pound twenty five pence) and it's yours, mate,' the trader bawled back.

'Let's have it,' Bryn said. 'We'll call back later for it and take it back by train. We needn't stay for the cinema.'

We left the market and crossed over to walk through the abbey precincts to have a cup of tea at Hands Dairy then made our way back to collect our bulky purchase. Taking an end each we carted it down to the railway station and attracted quite a bit of attention as we did.

Paris was to be the destination for our honeymoon and we decided to book with the Paris Travel Service. They arranged the complete package for us; all we had to do was book a train to London so we were there in time for the early morning boat train. We looked on Bryn's Paris plan to see where our hotel was and started saving spending money to take. There was a limit on how much currency you could take out of the country so there was not much point aiming for a higher target than the permitted twenty pounds.

I wanted to look fashionable on my first trip abroad and went shopping for accessories to wear with my cream coat. Emerald green! That was the colour! It came to me in a flash of inspiration. Something to give a zing to the subdued coat was needed and I had the confidence to stand out in a crowd. After trawling

Our wedding day 18th September 1965.
Outside the Montville Hotel, Mum, Bryn me and Dad.

from shop to shop at last I found the objects of my desire: gloves, handbag and suede shoes, all in brilliant emerald. Without hesitation I handed over my money and passed the bag to Bryn to carry. I had not finished yet.

I realised I did not have anything very stylish to wear under my coat and I could not keep it on for ever! I made for a rather more trendy shop; I did not want a department store garment. I soon settled on a dress that I thought no one else would have. It was designed by Mary Quant and was in charcoal grey flannel with a fine white pin stripe. The V-neck was edged in wide binding which was mirrored by the low slung, hip hugging belt. Sitting slap bang in the middle of the belt was a big black and white target with a tiny bullseye in the middle. It would look stunning with the emerald green accessories, I just needed a black polo necked jumper to go with it. Sighing happily I mentally checked my outfit and thought that even in fashionable Paris I would be able to hold my head high and be admired.

We made our way back to the station and loaded the parcels onto the luggage rack of our compartment.

The last few weeks of our engagement passed without any hitches. We had planned everything carefully and left nothing to chance. We had seen each other every single day for a year and worked together on our wedding plans and on our future home. Bryn and I had become used to the walk to Greenland Mills down Bridge Street and the tree-lined lane and as the summer sun sparkled through the trees we willed the days to pass more quickly to bring our wedding closer. Little did I guess that our dreamed-of marriage was only to last twenty years. Our love was gradually soured by the constant drip, drip effect of my mother's negativity and our hopes and aspirations were marred by, amongst other things, my involvement in the Women's Movement and my altered perception of life.

But that was in the future and for now we thought that no-one had ever been so in love as us and each day brought us closer to the fulfilment of that love: our wedding day.